Received On:

AUG 0 1 2014

Ballard Branch

The Artist on the Island

About the Author

Pete Hogan is a well known visual artist, who specialises in paintings of cityscape and seascape. Born in Ireland and educated at Cistercian College, Roscrea, Trinity College Dublin and Vancouver College of Art. He has travelled extensively. He is married to Micaela and they have two children, Clara and Joshua.

In 2012 Pete released his much-acclaimed *The Log of the Molly B* which describes his days as a boat bum when he sailed solo around the world by way of Cape Horn in a boat which he built himself.

Pete Hogan has exhibited his paintings with many groups and galleries over the years. His work is contained in several public and corporate collections, and countless private collections all over the world. For more information on Pete and his work see www. phogan.com.

THE ARTIST ON THE ISLAND

An Achill Journal

*Written and Illustrated
by Pete Hogan*

The Liffey Press

Published by
The Liffey Press Ltd
Raheny Shopping Centre, Second Floor
Raheny, Dublin 5, Ireland
www.theliffeypress.com

A catalogue record of this book is
available from the British Library.

ISBN 978-1-908308-49-8

Printed in Spain by GraphyCems.

Contents

Acknowledgements

I would like to thank the following people who helped to get this book off the ground: David Givens of The Liffey Press for encouragement and design work. Clare Ambrose for help and advice. Also Felicity McCartan, Jim Quigley, Aodh Bourke and Micaela Kuh.

I consulted the work of many authors during the writing of this book. Especially I would like to acknowledge the following: Jonathan Beaumont, *Achillbeg: The Life of an Island*; Theresa McDonald, *Achill Island*; Anne Chambers, *Granuaile: Grace O'Malley – Ireland's Pirate Queen*; S.B. Kennedy, *Paul Henry*; and Gordon T. Ledbetter. *Privilege and Purgatory: A Life of Alexander Williams RHA*.

A big thank you to all the many people who helped me when I stayed on Achillbeg. It seems like it was only yesterday.

This book is dedicated to the people of Achill and Corraun

Achillbeg Island

Achillbeg Island is a small island situated on the south side of the main island of Achill, County Mayo. It guards the south end of Achill Sound, a narrow, fast running tidal stretch of water linking Clew Bay in the south to Blacksod Bay in the north. Midway along the sound there is a bridge linking Achill Island to the mainland. Here is located the village named Achill Sound.

Achillbeg is an island of about 300 acres. Once, in pre-famine times, it might have supported a busy population of 200 souls but that gradually dwindled to a handful of families by the early 1960s. At this point the islanders decided to abandon the harsh life of their island. They moved to the neighbouring larger island of Achill, to Corraun on the mainland or further afield. That was in 1965. Achillbeg, its houses, walls, fields, roads, drains, school, wells, beaches, and cliffs have remained untouched since the islanders departed. At least 500 sheep graze out a living on the island. A half dozen or so of the houses have been sold and renovated as holiday homes, and it was in one such house that I stayed on Achillbeg for a winter.

This book is presented in the form of a journal and I stick closely to a chronological format. It is based on the journal which I kept at the time, the winter of 1982, and expanded with more contemporaneous observations. The illustrations are mostly recent but many are based on sketches, ideas and observations I made at the time.

There is an entry for every day I spent on the island. I hope the reader does not find this tedious. This practice produces a certain transparency and openness. There is nowhere to hide, a sort of writing equivalent of *Big Brother* and reality TV. I could not make this up, the chronology, the narrative and the detail. If I tried, I think it would be obvious.

This keeping of journals seems to have been a time honoured practice of my heroes, the travel writers and adventurers who I read – Bill Tilman, Dervla Murphy, Bruce Chatwin. The lone traveller fills the long evenings by writing in their journal. Be they in a Parisian café, in a yurt on the slopes of the Himalayan mountains or in some windswept anchorage, the book writes itself.

There is one big difference between the Achillbeg of the present and that of thirty years ago. There were very few channels of communication – no mobile phones! To communicate with the pier

at Cloghmore about a mile away you had to go there. To speak to Westport, 30 miles away, you had to get to a telephone, the nearest one being three miles away, and hope that it was working and that you had the right combination of loose change in your pocket. Then, if the operator was available, you might get through. To get in touch with Dublin, writing a letter seemed the best option. The mobile phone has changed all that. Now a friend can call or text, arrange to be met at the pier at Cloghmore and brought into the island. If they are delayed or change their mind – no problem.

Had the local people stayed on Achillbeg life would have become much easier. In the way that it has changed many things, the communication revolution has changed the way of life on islands.

Recently, also, boats have become more reliable and commonplace. Plastic boats, inflatables, even kayaks are lighter, stronger and cheaper. The famed traditional currach is now covered in fibreglass rather than the tar and canvas of before. Outboard motors are now more reliable, lighter and powerful. Gone are the romantic days of oily struggles with a two horsepower Seagull outboard.

The Achill region has always fascinated because it is an island even though it has been attached by a bridge for many years. There are many parts of Mayo which are just as beautiful, as wild and desolate but they get much less attention. The mere fact of being an island seems to define Achill's identity and attract visitors, commentators and outsiders. There have been many down through the years who have left reports of natural wild beauty, animal life and the poverty of the inhabitants. These are the three common threads running through any record. The history of Achill is invariably sad, tragic and unhappy, not unlike the history of Mayo and Connaught in general. One searches in vain for any high points, any joyous occasions. Their wars were never merry and their wonderful songs are not always sad.

Why did I end up there? A combination of factors which are explained in the book goes some way to answering this. That is, if one needs a reason to be in the wonderful west of Ireland. A book is perhaps a rationale for the odd behaviour we sometimes find ourselves engaged in. Nothing much happens, but it might, if we leave ourselves open to it.

I had fled Ireland almost ten years earlier, first to work on luxury yachts in Florida, then to work in a paper company in Canada, a 'good' job. Two years later I had paid my dues to the real world. I retired, forever, and followed my dreams, like many before me, out to the west coast. To the clean air and water of British Columbia I went. In the true spirit of 'go west young man' I had quit my job and driven across Canada to build the 30-foot ketch *Molly B* in a derelict warehouse in Vancouver. I set sail in the engineless *Molly B* and

headed south. Passing along the coast of the United States, Mexico and Central America, I came to the Panama Canal. I persuaded a friendly yacht to tow me through to the Atlantic side. I stopped in Florida. Then, in an epic, 40-day voyage, using a school atlas for a chart and the sun for navigation, I crossed the Atlantic and landed on Achillbeg Island, County Mayo, Ireland. I felt I had come home.

I was not in the mood for compromise. I wanted to live on an island and make art. If Paul Gauguin could quit his job as a stockbroker and paint pictures on an island in the middle of the Pacific ocean, so could I, but in the west of Ireland. If James Joyce could be an exile in Trieste and 'forge in the smithy of his soul the uncreated conscience of his race', then so could I, but on an island in the west of Ireland. If

Andy Warhol could become famous from some nightclub in New York, then so could I, but on an island in the west of Ireland. I would be famous, aloof, celebrated and revered – from an island in the west of Ireland.

Or so I thought. I parked my engineless, gaff-rigged ketch. I unloaded my dreams. I kicked open the door of the house and I settled in. I kept a journal that winter. What follows is based on what I wrote.

Chapter 1

Grass to the Knee

I will bring you, my kine,
Where there's grass to the knee;
But you'll think of scant croppings
Harsh with salt of the sea.
– Padraig Colum

Wednesday, September 22, 1982

Achillbeg is settling down for the winter. One could almost say 'at last' because for the past two months it has been a bit hectic. There has been a constant stream of people visiting the house here. There had also been many other visitors to the other inhabited houses on the island. Day trippers, picnickers, relatives, friends, friends of friends, returned islanders, campers, divers, canoeists, workmen and walkers. Not that one is really complaining, but now they have all gone, leaving the island to the sheep and to myself.

The last to go was Mrs. Boydell. She left on Monday presenting me with some fine sprouts, cabbage and apples. The sprouts and the cabbage she has grown on the island. She lives in London where

among other things she rears red-haired sheep. She also makes pottery and, of course, fires it in a wood-burning kiln. She is also very musical being from a musical family. She is all into 'self-sufficiency'. In fact, she puts me to shame. She has no electricity connection to her house on the island, grows her own vegetables and saves her own turf from a small bog on the island. She then cooks on her turf fire. She runs about the island in her bare feet looking for mushrooms. She riles against the fast buck merchants who would develop Achillbeg into a package holiday resort. As if there was much chance of that. She has gone back to London in her little minivan.

Molly B has been anchored off the beach for the last month or so. Yesterday I brought her around from the beach anchorage to the slip, which is the landing place on Achillbeg. On the top of the tide I ran her up as high as I could on the steep, shale shore. As the tide went out she keeled over and dried out. I took the masts out of her and unshipped the rudder. All part of my plan to lay *Molly* B up for the winter.

I got a shock today when I went down to inspect the beached *Molly B.* When the tide went out, the fat dumpy hull, balancing on

its thick, long keel was left standing upright like a wine glass. This was a dangerous situation. The hull could fall over on to someone or on to a rock and be damaged. Luckily, it was not too windy. A strong wind might be enough to do the deed. The tight anchor and shore lines were helping to keep the hull upright and stable. There was nothing for it but to leave the situation in balance, hope for the best and await the incoming tide.

I spent most of the day working in the house on a couple of entries for the Castlebar International Song Contest Art Competition. I had seen an ad for it in the *Mayo News*. While in the midst of this (happily I was not in bed or anything like that), I received a visit from the Achill Sound gardaí. A sergeant and a guard knocked on the door. 'Just a routine check on the island,' they said. They thought I had just arrived. Or so they said. Presumably there might be some connection between beaching the boat around at the slip and the visit. This is the first time I have ever seen a guard on the

island. I have never even heard of any gardaí activity on Achilllbeg. I offered them a beer, which they accepted, and we had some small talk but things were slightly strained. They seemed to be a bit on the defensive, even embarrassed, as, Sherlock Holmes-like, they figured there was nothing much amiss here. No drugs, no guns, no undersize nets. Not even a woman! Then off they went. I wonder how they got on to the island. Somebody must have put them up to it.

I returned to the free standing *Molly B* in the evening with the incoming tide. She was still upright as the water crept slowly up to the waterline. I slacked off one of the shorelines and *Molly B* fell gently over into deep water, safe. Then I carried the mizzen mast about a quarter of the way up to the house. The masts, basically grown trees, are heavy.

Weather is getting blustery with some sunny spells.

Thursday, September 23

I got all excited about the Castlebar International Song Contest Art Competition, with its £150 worth of prizes. I framed two paintings nicely and today brought them over to Castlebar. One was a conventional landscape and the other a more intimate picture of the interior of *Molly B.*

Transportation to Castlebar is not as straight forward as one might think. It's a good illustration of the problems of living on this island. The paintings had to be well packaged and protected against water damage. I lugged them down to the slip and shipped them across to the pier at Cloghmore in the punt. The punt, a 14-foot wooden open boat with a small outboard motor, is my link with the outside world. I then hitched the two miles to Achill Sound with the pictures under my arm in time to connect with the bus to Westport. This bus passes through Newport. Luckily, it was dry and sunny and I got a lift from Pattens pub to the Sound, helping to make sure I caught the bus. There is no direct link with Castlebar. I have to connect with the train in Westport.

I had a nice pub meal in the Imperial Hotel in Castlebar then delivered my masterpieces. I did some shopping and visited the library. I met an aunt on the street in Castlebar. 'You're terrible not to call in and see us,' she says. The hinterland is full of my relations. A fecund bunch they are. I then returned to the island the way I had come, managing to hitch a lift from Achill Sound to Cloghmore. A full day, I thought. Two pictures exported, and a sure thing for third prize at the Castlebar International Song Contest Art Competition. They will give the first prize to the local favourite, second prize to an up and coming young star and third to the whacky Artist on the Island who was recently in the *Mayo News*. Or so I figured.

Chapter 2

A Fire in My Head

I went out to the hazel wood,
Because a fire was in my head,
And cut and peeled a hazel wand,
And hooked a berry to a thread ...
– W.B. Yeats

How did I get here? If you have read *The Log of the Molly B* you will have a fair idea. I had built the 30-foot double-ended gaff ketch in Vancouver, British Columbia. I had sailed her through the Panama Canal, up to Florida and across the Atlantic stopping in the Aran Islands. All on a shoestring budget, using celestial navigation and without a motor. From the Aran Islands it was a short hop north around Slyne Head to the anchorage at Achillbeg.

The small island of Achillbeg had slowly seeped into my life. I first visited it in the late 1960s, shortly after the islanders had decided to move off the island to Achill and Corraun. Two uncles bought houses on Achillbeg which they used as holiday homes and lent out freely. I played on the beach with cousins and friends. We swam, built dams in the stream, made sandcastles. I climbed all over the island. To the top of its two mountains, down its cliffs to its hidden coves. Salvaged treasure on its beaches and acted like a king. Fished

for mackerel and potted for lobster. Used illegal nets in a vain hope of catching the elusive salmon. More *Swiss Family Robinson*, less *Lord of the Flies*.

The boats were leaky, the engines did not work, the tide was always against us. It was a struggle to get back and forth, but that was the fun and the magic. The card games lasted all night – Penny Poker and Slippery Sam. I always lost. The fire never went out, no one was excluded. We lived out of a frying pan and on biscuits. We were unsupervised and safe. We skinny dipped on the beach in the mid-summer moonlight, built up roaring turf fires and talked and sang long into the night.

Drinking started. I don't know where we got the money. Or the transport. The pubs on Achill were famous for late opening. The northerners arrived around the time of the Glorious Twelfth. It was before the time of the package tour to Spain.

Driving back in the middle of the night from 'Down the Island' the boat was high and dry, the hull leaky. The moon was full. We took off our shoes and socks, rolled up our trousers, pushed the heavy hull across the soft mud. We piled in with groceries and bottles. We pushed with the oars through the shallows. The oars broke, the motor would not start. Is there any petrol? Must be the carburettor. Somebody do some bailing. Do we have a bailer?

We paddled across and abandoned ship as we hit the beach. Somebody get the anchor. The sheep scattered in the moonlight as we struggled up the path. The dark gable walls silhouetted against the skyline. There, in the distance, was a light. The door crashes open. Somebody get the fire. Anyone for poker? Did ya bring the milk? What about some fried potatoes? Ah jeepers, we forgot the butter.

The mid-summer dawn started to break above Corraun. Where's Pete? He's no good, he's fallen asleep. Anyone for a swim?

'That was a good night,' we used to say. The postmortem.

I returned with a bunch of friends from college. We were interested in scuba diving. It was the middle of winter, the weather was terrible but as students with a lot of new diving gear to try out it was a free place to stay and the possibility of diving in the un-spoilt Atlantic. We rowed across in the leaky punt and huddled around the fire in the driving rain.

I had girlfriends. What a place to bring a girlfriend! An uninhabited island. How cool was that? It was the 1970s. The 1970s in Ireland were like the 1960s anywhere else. I cannot really remember what happened next . . .

Jim was always there. He was the man. Tall, dark, cool, he had a boat which did not leak and a motor which worked, quite a thing in those days. He brought me out to Clare Island to visit his friends. There was the famous, late, Michael Joe O'Malley who I feel privileged to have met. A true renaissance man he wanted to talk about philosophy, sheep, poitín and eastern religions. He listened all night to BBC Radio 4. Serious stuff. He had a saying which he put into practice. 'If you just stay in one place, the world will come to you.' And the world did come to Clare Island to Michael Joe O'Malley. RIP.

Not far from Michael Joe's house, up at the disused lighthouse, there was a budding artist's commune. Everyone was welcome in the unrenovated, abandoned lighthouse. An American had bought the old lighthouse when the light moved to Achillbeg. His son was a budding photographer. He had plans to turn the lighthouse into a photo museum, archive, lab, gallery. Big ideas that grew with the lateness of the hour and the substances consumed. It did not happen, but not for want of late night planning. A well-thumbed copy of Henry David Thoreau's *Walden* was passed around. I did not realise then that it might have an influence on me many years later when I came to stay on Achillbeg.

Down at the Clare Island harbour, below Granuaile's tower house, was a shop, a post office and most important of all, a pub. We drank out on the streets, swam in the harbour, lay in the sun. We lit a fire on the beach, cooked our mackerel and ate it off flat stones. Then we sailed back to our island. We were 18 years old and masters of the universe.

On Achillbeg, the house had no windows or door. Four rooms, the floors covered in sheep droppings. The wind blowing through broken glass. Slates coming off the roof, plaster off the walls, swallows nesting in the eaves, gutters gone. The owner was living in Birmingham. He was willing to sell. The deal was done.

I was sailing up the Thames estuary in an 18-foot open boat with my friend Drewry at the time. As we arrived at Tower Bridge I got the call. 'I bought a house on Achillbeg. Will you come back and do it up?' asked my mother. Drewry lost a crew, but in truth, after a long summer in France together, we were ready for a break.

John Welsh, in Westport, had just returned from London. There he had built, among other things, London Airport. He wanted to settle down in his home town and was keen to work. He came out to Achillbeg with his measuring tape and made a long list of materials. Uncle Vincent filled his launch from the hardware shops in Westport. In one 30-mile trip from Westport Quay across the bay he arrived at Achillbeg beach. He ran the launch up on the beach like a D-Day landing craft. Cement and wood, pipes and gutters, chipboard and nails, light fixtures and wires came tumbling out. Like the pioneer wagons crossing the prairies we landed the lot on the beach at Achillbeg. The windows and front door, made in beautiful hardwood, came from a workshop in Louisburg across the bay.

We set to work with a will, family and friends helping John Welsh. Plumbing, plastering, wiring, roofing and glazing – John could do it all. We were the helpers. We lived in Uncle Geoffrey's house on sausages, lobsters and digestive biscuits. We plugged an illegal wire into the nearby electricity line, a dangerous and foolish

thing to do. We worked long into the night. The weather was on our side, a magnificent Indian summer. John had given a 'price'. He was a good man and his work stands to this day.

Vincent was everyone's favourite uncle. He was never happier than when spending a day out 'on the bay', fishing and landing on an island. He knew all the islands of Clew Bay by name. And there are 365 of them, as everyone knows. His pride and joy was the *St Ann*, a North Mayo fishing boat he had converted to an angling boat for Clew Bay. He had installed his favorite Lister diesel and built a cabin. It was in this launch that he delivered the building materials to Achillbeg. He was amused rather than censorious of my decision to spend a winter there and helped in whatever way he could.

From the Aran Islands to Achill is a short hop across the wind for a sailing boat. It would be shorter were it not for the obstacle of Slyne Head, which juts out resolutely into the Atlantic in a series of islands. The currents run strong around Slyne Head and it always has to be respected.

Molly B rounded Slyne Head in fine weather and with a prevailing southwest breeze. A ship of the Irish navy, one of the old Flower class corvettes, passed close by, checking me out. No doubt headed north to supervise the Donegal salmon fishery. I waved. They waved back from the bridge. I had no VHF radio. I dipped the Canadian flag on the back stay of *Molly B*. I waited. A small figure could be seen climbing down an exterior ladder from the bridge. He walked back along the side deck, past the gun and the other equipment on the aft deck. He hauled down the Irish tricolour and slowly raised it back up in salute. YES! Good old Irish Navy. Good old traditions of the sea.

It would have been nice to have sailed across the Atlantic and landed on Achillbeg directly. It would have been a statement. But there were practical considerations against such a course. I felt I had to enter Ireland at a 'Port of Entry' to go through customs. In any case, I was happy to hit Ireland anywhere with my dodgy navigation

and school atlas chart. So I had made my landfall on Loop Head and stopped at the Aran Islands.

I sailed on past Innisboffin, past the dramatic coast of Connemara in the distance inshore, past High Island, Killary Harbour, Innishturk, some smaller isles and then the bulk of Clare Island. Three miles further on was the clear water and sand of the anchorage at Achillbeg. I had arrived.

Achillbeg is a fine island. For a start, it has some height, two rocky hills of over 100 meters each, joined by a lowland divide. Perhaps 20 houses, it might, at its height, have sustained 200 souls. It has arable land, good water, no trees, little bog and a couple of well sheltered boat landing spots. A fine sandy beach sheltered from the west. It has a school house, an Iron Age promontory fort and a holy well.

Achillbeg is very close to Achill Island itself. Perhaps not that long ago it was connected. At low spring tides people can wade across the Blind Sound where the land bridge would have been. I have never done so. Or drive animals across. But most of the time it is a true island, cut off from the main by strong, dangerous currents.

This was August and Achillbeg was in her summer mode with a few of the houses occupied and people coming and going, usually to the beach. I sailed up to Westport to greet the relatives and show-off the boat. The *Mayo News* made a big deal of my transatlantic voyage, putting a picture of me on the front page. They were keen to spin the story as an emigrant's return.

Sailing inside the islands of Clew Bay in the engineless *Molly B* is a hit and miss affair. More hit than miss in the shallow waters and strong currents. But it is very safe. *Molly B* takes going aground in her stride like the hookers of old, no doubt, did. An inconvenience rather than a hazard.

So I used up the balmy days of summer taking relatives out for day trips and eating home-cooked meals. It was good to have a decent shower in a clean bathroom. They were insulted when I would not use their guest bedrooms and spare beds but stayed on *Molly B*. She had been my home for at least three years. I headed back through the maze of islands, against the prevailing winds, to Achillbeg.

Neil and his girlfriend, Nora, visited. We went for a sail around Clare Island. They gave me a copy of a wonderful book which turned out to be almost a template for my stay on Achillbeg. The book was J.M. Synge's *The Aran Islands*.

Chapter 3

Turf

I will arise and go now, and go to Innisfree,
And a small cabin build there, of clay and wattles made;
Nine bean rows will I have there, a hive for the honeybee,
And live alone in the bee-loud glade.
— W.B. Yeats

Friday, September 24

The turf has arrived. A full trailer load hauled by a tractor. It has been dumped right at the water's edge in the car park beside the pier at Cloghmore. From there it can be easily loaded into the punt for the trip across to the island.

Achillbeg Island has very little exploitable turf and the islanders had, in the past, cut and saved their turf at the far end of the sound in the townland of Saile. Turf, as vital to the island economy as oil is to our modern one, must have been one of the major preoccupations of the Achillbeg year. Cut in the spring, dried, hopefully, over the early summer it would then be transported by boat down the sound on the tide to be landed and stacked on Achillbeg. Thus had naturally evolved the local sailing vessels – the Achill yawls. Using the sound as a natural waterway and working the tides and winds, the winter's supply of turf was transported to Achillbeg.

Probably adapted from the local coastguard boats with their dipping lugsails, the yawls are still a sight on Achill Sound. As the Galway hookers in the south brought cargo, including vast quantities of turf, to the Aran Islands, so the Achill yawls were used to service Achillbeg.

I did not have an Achill yawl, though I seriously thought of trying to get one. But I did have my 14-foot punt and outboard motor to do the job.

I never seriously considered cutting and saving my own turf. Apart from anything else, like the necessary expertise, it is a long drawn out process involving cutting, drying and saving over the spring/summer season. I was more into instant gratification when it came to turf. I bought a load and had it dumped at Cloghmore. Now I had to get it over to the island.

Saturday, September 25

Yesterday I got two boat loads of turf across to Achillbeg and stacked at the slip. It should be possible to get three boatloads across in one tide. There are about four boatloads left. I am planning to leave the bulk of the turf at the slip and bring it up to the house as needed. The wheelbarrow lift to the house, an uphill, bumpy ride

of about a mile, is slow going, especially with the heavy builder's wheelbarrow which I have borrowed.

Today was windy and I was happy to have the excuse not to bring any more turf across the choppy water of the sound. The wind increased from the south and southwest to gale force by afternoon.

I did some repairs to the road down to the slip with a pick and shovel, unblocking the drains and building up the bank where it had eroded away. It is a well-engineered track which would have been used for donkey and horse carts for many years. No one has done any maintenance on the road since the islanders left some twenty years previously. As the road skirts a cliffy section, when the drain fails, the road collapses down the cliff, eroded by the incessant, errant water. The path remains but has to detour around the numerous landfalls.

Like the terraces of the Mediterranean lands or the rice paddies of the east, the walls and roads of the west of Ireland are a tribute and a reminder of the energy and latent industry of the original inhabitants. Achillbeg is no different and the walls remain even though the people are gone. They are damaged and flattened in many places, but will never be obliterated. Like the walls of Troy or the nearby Céide Fields, they endure.

An hour or so of hacking away at blocked drains with a pick and shovel was enough for me. The job is Sisyphean. I abandon it. I think it is going to take a bigger resident community to maintain the roads and walls than this island's sole inhabitant.

In the afternoon a boatload of sheep farmers came in from Corraun and brought off about 60 lambs which a buyer had come over to purchase. Presumably they would be the lambs which had been born that spring. I went over to see them and say hello. The men were a wild looking bunch, with the hard work, the beer they were drinking and the excitement of the sale. It must be a big day for the hard working sheep men to finally get some return from all the long, yearly slog of tending and minding the sheep.

I spoke to the buyer, a more prosperous looking fellow. I had noticed a lamb with short back feet hobbling around the island and asked about it. He said he had bought it. It will be slaughtered along with the rest and end up on a table. That's life, if you are a mountainy black-faced lamb.

To get the lambs down to the shore from the pens, the sheep men straddle the lambs with their legs, hold them firmly by the horns and walk them forcibly where they want to go. Then they throw them quite a distance into the boat like a sack of sand. They do this by holding them, one hand on a horn and one hand on the rump and up in the air they go. To unload them on the other side at Corraun they dump them into the shallow water and let them wade ashore. It's a messy business for the farmer.

The sheep farmers do not take much notice of me. It's an important day for them, I presume, and I feel a bit of an interloper as I watch.

I lit a fire in the house early today, for the first time, as the weather gets colder. I leave it smoldering away with a kettle of water over it on a hook to provide a hot water supply in addition to the hot water I have on tap. I am reading Paul Henrys *Further Reminiscences* which I managed to get in the library in Castlebar. Paul Henry wrote two books. His first, and best, *An Irish Portrait*, deals extensively with his time in Achill.

Sunday, September 26

It's a nice day with the wind dying out overnight. The sun is shining. Sunday means Mass. I'm not that committed, but I am a Catholic. It's a cultural thing and an opportunity to connect with the community.

I got a leisurely start and motored up the sound with the tide to the church at Dereens, about a mile from Cloghmore. You can only do that in the punt when the timing of the tide suits. I was unfortunately 15 minutes late for Mass having made a mistake about the time. I walked the short distance to Patten's pub and shop for a newspaper after Mass. 'I thought you'd gone,' they said in the pub. They all know me but I'm not really able to figure out who most of them are and the names are a real problem. Stupidly, I mumbled in reply, 'Yes I have. Up top.' I ran back to the boat and cast off for a pleasant motor back into the island. In Achill, and other parts of the west, you go 'into' an island, not 'over to' or 'on to'.

I was just finishing breakfast when Michael and Tom Gallagher and a friend came past. Young lads, out for a walk to see the island where their parents were born. About an hour later I remembered

my masts at the bottom of the hill and had an idea. I ran after them and got them to help me bring the two masts up to the house. A nice little job done as the main mast is quite a weight.

I feed the masts in through the gable end window of the house. They just fit, stretching from the main dividing wall of the house to the window in the gable end, a distance of about thirty feet. They pass through the door of the back bedroom and so that door now has to remain open. I have to dodge under them presently to get into my bed, but I should be able to rearrange things so that they are up higher in the air out of the way. I hang my clothes and towels on them. They were cut down by me in the forests of British Columbia. They powered me across the Atlantic. They are shiny and worn from the rubbing of the ropes and sails. Now they are a towel rail for the winter!

Excitement of the day was when I saw some choughs. Mrs. Boydell had been waxing lyrical about the choughs. She claims they are rare. I had never heard of choughs, I had to admit to her. I think that succeeded in making her feel intellectually superior. As she explained, they are big black/blue shiny birds with fabulous big red beaks and legs. Thus the name – the 'red-billed chough'. Apparently they mate for life. One was sharpening his beak on a big stone outside the door and its mate was pecking about around it. They moved off after a few minutes, complaining loudly. They are renowned for their loud call. 'Breaking the silence of the seas.'

Monday, September 27

A good solid work day. Up at 8.30 and got a business letter typed. I have my trusty old typewriter and lots of correction fluid. Business letters involve writing to anyone and everyone and asking them for money in exchange for art and/or proposing wacky arty schemes. I am a Man of Letters. The Artist on the Island. The letters will be collected, treasured, donated to colleges and museums, published in anthologies, quoted in biographies and learned theses. If you get one you are a fortunate, important person. Hopefully, you will respond by becoming a patron of the Artist on the Island.

I made a crude Achillbeg letterhead out of a piece of wood. A wood block print. I used this on the top of my letters printed in all shades of coloured paint.

Then I installed a plexiglas screen on top of the west end window of the house. This was the window through which I had fed the two masts. Being on the west end gable of the house, that window takes most battering from the wind and rain. The plexiglass will give the window some insulation. A good job, well done, using non-ferrous screws. This will prevent the driven rain from getting in the window. Sort of crude double glazing.

I walked down to the slip and met Sean O Malley from Corraun, the man who looks after the lighthouse and a member of a highly regarded boat-building family. I showed him around *Molly B* which is beached nearby. He is, sort of, a silent type. He didn't say much about my dream ship.

Then over to Cloghmore and brought off a load of turf. Unloaded it at the slip and went back for a second. I met old Mr Kilbane, who

said, 'I haven't long in it.' He lives in the house above the pier at Cloghmore. He was the first to row us into the island many years ago. He had taught me early about the tidal currents, shallows and back eddies which could be used as one crossed the sound. The different, safe routes to take at various stages of the tide.

I got the second load of turf over and went back up to the house for lunch. By this time it was about 4.00 in the afternoon. Then back down to the slip and unloaded the second load from the boat. I have piled all the turf up in a nice pyramid well above the high water tide line. Work was completed and back to the house by about 8.00 p.m. It looks as though there will be six boatloads of turf when I have brought it all across. There are about ten to twelve wheelbarrow loads of turf in each boatload.

I loaded the turf into the punt a bit higher today than I did on the previous days. A little bit too much weight on board. On the turn of the tide a chop developed with the wind blowing against the current. For a time I feared that the bow of the punt might go under as we motored across through the chop. If that happened it would be a disaster. The punt would fill, sink and the motor would be destroyed.

The turf would be gone. Turf floats and it would drift off up Clew Bay. The embarrassment would be the worst. I could swim ashore.

But I slowed right down. The bow stayed above the waves and we came through without mishap. I had hoped to get three loads over to the island today and one probably could on a spring tide when there would be more time. But the tides are presently in neap phase. Everything on Achillbeg is connected with the tide, controlled by the tide, conscious of the tide.

Tuesday, September 28

It was a wild, windy night. I tend to wake up before dawn and watch the light in the window as it gets brighter. It creeps into the living room revealing the face of the clock on the mantelpiece, the faintly smoldering fire, the cement floor and the streaky, yellowing whitewash on the walls. I give myself an extra few minutes. The days are getting shorter. It's not that much colder but it seems harder to get up early. The lack of light as winter sets in is not an inducement.

I did a mushroom gathering walk. They grow in patterns in particular places. I head over to the beach and up to the plateau on which sits the Paorachs house. I only find two mushrooms. The mushrooms are ending. It was a good year for mushrooms this year but it is getting late in the season. The crop varies from year to year.

I had the fire going early to take the bite out of the air. I tend to linger over the dismal, smoking fire and wear a woolly hat in the house. I did a laundry in the bath. The house has hot and cold running water, the only such convenience on the entire island. The hot water is provided by a giant immersion heater which is supplied from the well. All mod cons. Then I went down to the slip to check on all my boats, the *Molly B*, its tender and the punt. The wind has been very strong. The boats were OK.

I did some carving in the afternoon. I am working on the 'Angel of the Lord' from my nativity set. Auntie Clare has ordered a

carved nativity set from me. Almost my first patron. I bought the wood for it in San Diego – a nice piece of Honduras mahogany. I have been working on the commission on and off for the last year. It's an interesting and enjoyable carving which appears to be coming together well. The angel's harp is from the Irish coinage. She (it's a female angel) has a sword, sort of butterfly wings and a Mary Quant hairdo. Looks like it could be a maquette for Eamon de Valera's tomb. I did a bit of a clean-up on my chisels. The damp air is hard on good tools. I lather them with copious quantities of grease and oil.

Achillbeg is an ideal place for a carving studio. That had always been in the back of my mind. There is not a chance in the world that anyone will be disturbed by the noise or the dust which carving inevitably entails.

Wednesday, September 29

Woke up with a sore throat, a slight headache and pains in my neck. Perhaps I have made the back room, where I installed the double glazing, too stuffy. It's a slow moving day and I went back to bed in the afternoon. I fixed some of the gutter on the roof which is falling down and did a tar caulking job on the front door to stop draughts. Any draughts, of which there are many, are becoming very noticeable and irritating as the weather gets colder.

I went down to the slip thinking I might go over and explore Corraun on the top of the tide, but did not feel up to it and changed my mind. It's a nice day, weather-wise. There'll be fun if I do get seriously sick or cut myself. Some people will say, 'I told you so'.

Thursday, September 30

I have a long lie-in in the morning and felt a bit better when I did get up. I still have a sore throat. It's a windy, rainy day. A leak in the roof into the main room becomes apparent. That will have to be investigated.

The roof of the house is pretty basic. Dating from the 1930s, it consists of the standard, vernacular, artificial slates of the time. There

is no insulation. Under the slates is a slathering of crumbly mortar roughly troweled on. Under that, visible from inside the house, there is an attractive layer of thin pine planks, painted in some rooms, stained in others. That's it.

A previous generation of houses on Achillbeg would have been thatched. This would have provided better insulation. The houses also would have been smaller with much lower roofs. They would have been easier to heat with the smoldering turf fires.

When the wind blows, the roof starts to rattle. In a gale the noise can be quite loud. Like a Boeing revving up for take-off. As the slates flex in the wind they let in a lot of air. They also rub against the nails which hold them to the wooden roof laths. Over time the nails corrode and wear through. Or a slate breaks in two from all the vibration. Half the slate falls out and the rain trickles in. The half of the slate remaining on the roof is difficult to remove and thus prevents the installation of a replacement. In addition, the vibration of the slates causes the weak mortar to crumble off in light, sandy dust. This falls on the wooden laths beneath and works its way through the gaps in the laths. It falls into the room on to its contents and inhabitants below. This constant snowfall of dusty mortar increases as the wind does.

I am a dab hand at replacing a fallen slate. There is a trick for doing this. Using a battery of improvised tools, like specially shaped flat scrapers and pullers and hack saws, the remains of the broken slate is removed. A stopper made up of a strip of lead is installed and a new slate slid up into place. Job done. Great care must be taken not to disturb the other slates which are in place, patiently doing their job for the last fifty or more years. An array of light roof ladders and a calm day is a *sine qua non* for this acrobatic job.

It's going to be a long, wet winter and I am getting ready for it.

Chapter 4

Manly Bearing

Now you're up on deck, you're a fisherman,
You can swear and show a manly bearin'
Take your turn on watch with the other fellows,
While you're searchin' for the shoals of herring
– Ewan MacColl

Saturday, October 2

I had a slowish day yesterday. Just getting over a cold and a sore throat. Went up to Pattens by boat in the afternoon on the flood tide. Pattens is the local pub, shop and post office. There is a phone box there. I dropped into Corraun harbour on the way back to take a look around. Corraun also has a pub, shop and post office.

I am interested in checking out the harbour as a place to store *Molly B*. The harbour in Corraun is a picturesque little enclave with great shelter. It dries out at half tide making it extra safe as a storage place. There is a boat building shed and all about are the hulls and hulks of wooden boats and currachs in various states of repair, storage and dereliction.

Back at the slip I took the bowsprit off *Molly B*. *Molly B* floats on the top of the high tides when it is at the slip. It is held in place bow

and stern by a series of taught anchor and shore lines. But the keel grinds badly on the beach as it floats off the bottom on each tide. Not good for the keel. I will have to move her on to an anchor or mooring, or into Corraun harbour, or else there will be no keel left on her at all come the summer. There can be quite a swell into the slip, especially today as big rollers break all the way across the entrance from Achillbeg to the rocks off Corraun. This is the bar at the south end of Achill Sound, though I do not think anyone calls it that. It is a shallow bank of sand deposited there by the strong tides running through the sound over the centuries.

Today I got up a head of steam and achieved a lot between art work, taking equipment off *Molly B* and bringing it up to the house, letter writing and carving. The Angel from the nativity set is pretty well in the bag, that is, finished. I had a nice bath in the evening and lit a big turf fire.

I'm getting very fond of the radio. In fact, it is becoming completely addictive. I need a guide so I can only listen to programmes of interest. The RTÉ Guide. The radio, which I took off *Molly B*, has only been up in the house for the past week but is dominating my existence.

Sunday, October 3

My uncle, Geoffrey, and two of his boys arrived to close up their house for the winter. Geoffrey came down to my house bringing a big tinned steak and kidney lunch for me. This laid me out for the rest of the day. Geoffrey advises me to leave *Molly B* where she is, at the slip. So now I don't know what to do with the boat. He gives me a big sack of food from his own house as he departs. I don't think he much approves of my plan to stay on the island, but he is helpful in this practical way. He is a solid Mayo man, living and working as a vet in Castlebar. He knows the ways of the county well. He had lent me his own house on Achillbeg countless times over the years.

I saw a fox today, near the house. It seemed to be mooching around, scavenging. The horse and goat nearby seemed undisturbed, as were the sheep, by its proximity. Unfortunately, just as I saw the fox two young visitors appeared nearby, walking the hill, so I had to

keep moving into the house so as not to draw attention to the fox. The fox ran down the hill, across the football pitch, past the school and up to its usual hide above the schoolhouse. The fox keeps its tail very low to the ground and the tail seems to be streaked with grey.

The fox pretty well completes the fauna of the island. About 500 sheep, a horse, a goat, rats, mice, seals, possibly some sea otters and lots of birds. There is talk that there are hares on the island from time to time but I have never seen one. Nor have I ever seen a bat despite the many empty ruins which they like to inhabit. On the sand hills and fields of Corraun there are many rabbits and they do much damage to the landscape. Luckily, they do not seem to have been able to make it over on to Achillbeg. Obviously they cannot swim.

I gaze across at Corraun, at the little white specks of cottages nestling under the sepia-coloured hill. It is quite a backwater, off the beaten track. At low tide a large area of rocky reef fronts the shore almost the whole way to Mulranny. An inhospitable exposed shore on to which a ship of the Spanish Armada is reputed to have foundered.

Monday, October 4

Down to the slip at 8.30, on the way doing some more work on the drainage of the road. And it is far from finished. Brought up my daily wheelbarrow load of turf. Then I had a marathon session in the workshop, reorganising it, improving the workbench and the kitchen table and moving in a chest of drawers for storage. That in itself would have been a good day's work. I also finished a frame and did some painting.

The house consists of four rooms plus a small kitchen and a cramped bathroom. The main room takes up the middle of the house and is dominated by a large fireplace. A large window to the front and a smaller one to the rear give good light. Off this main room to the west are two separate bedrooms. To the east, or sheltered side of the house, the original layout included a large bedroom. This bedroom has been partitioned into three to make a small kitchen and bathroom, and what's left remains a bedroom.

I commandeer the whole house and take the smallest, western bedroom at the back for sleeping. The front bedroom I convert into a workshop and the bedroom beside the kitchen I use for storage. It is the driest in the house. The main living room with its fireplace I use as a studio, dining room, sitting room and occasional bedroom. When the going gets cold I end up sleeping in it. Tacked on to the front of the house is a large porch which has wonderful light and a panoramic view out through two large windows. The kitchen is dominated by a bottled gas cooker, a sink and, luckily, a working

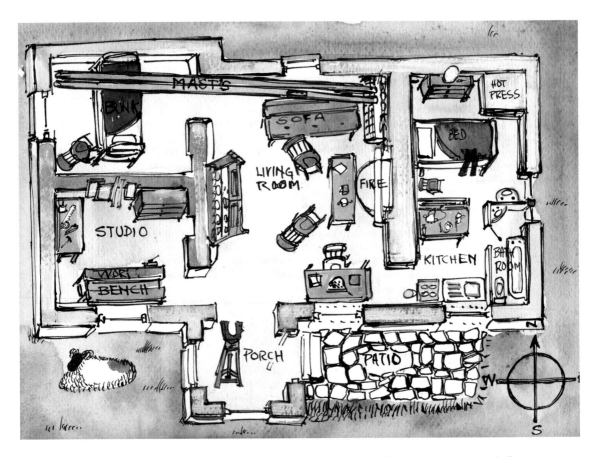

fridge. The bathroom, amazingly, contains a bath, probably, no, definitely, the only one on the island. Certainly, the only working one. There is also a loo and a small hand basin. This is to be my home for the winter.

I went down to the slip in the evening to *Molly B* to try to haul her further up the beach on the top of the tide.

Tuesday, October 5

Up early. That's about 8.00 a.m. at this time of the year. I headed out on a mushroom hunt and got four. They are nearly finished for the year I think.

Some house reorganisation. Cleaned out the porch which I intend to use mainly for finishing, that is, varnishing and some lumber storage. Found signs of rats in the east end bedroom. I ripped out the floor of the press there in search of the hole where they might have got in, but I think they came in via the front door. So did a bit of a job on bottom of front door. Went down to *Molly B* at the slip and ran a new aft line on an anchor out to the northwest. Also changed other lines and chaffing points around.

It's cold and windy with violent squalls and rain showers. Had fire smoldering all day but it is more for distraction than additional thermal output. On the plus side, looking at the house from a distance as I trudge over the fields, the smoke oozing out of the chimney is a cheerful, welcoming sight.

I seem to have eaten an incredible range of food today, my menu still being influenced by cooking habits imposed by living on board *Molly B* for so long, such as porridge, crackers, dried fruit and the eternal pancake. Here are today's meals:

9.30 a.m., breakfast – Porridge, bread, jam, tea, crackers, and raisins.

12.00, break – Coffee, crackers, cheese, jam, chocolate.

3.00 p.m., dinner – Bacon, sausages, egg, plate of granola, banana, tea, bread, jam.

5.00 p.m., Supper – Pancakes, tea, orange, granola, coffee.

This army marches on its stomach!

Wednesday, October 6

I have an active day getting across early on the top of the tide to Cloghmore for a load of turf. There is one small load remaining and that's all the turf to be transported across to the slip.

I met the Winkle Picker as he had his tea and a snack at the slip before setting out for the day's picking. He kindly offers me some cake. His father was a picker, he said. He gets £18 a hundredweight and can pick half that in a day. 'The price will hit £20 by Christmas,' he predicts. He enquired if the small dinghy of the *Molly B* might be

for sale, but I said no. I explained that it was an important part of the equipment as the yacht had no motor.

We talked about Mass. (I had seen him the previous Sunday in Corraun.) He lamented the change from Latin to English. 'It makes it too straightforward,' he said. They used to have the young priest, who is now in Dereens, in Corraun. He apparently says a fast Mass. 'The old priests are much slower,' he said. He doesn't have a TV. 'The license is too dear'. It's £40 for a colour one. He likes the radio. We had more chat. He seems a gentle, reserved sort but not afraid of saying hello to me.

There was other activity on the island. The sheep men were in and the young rams were being 'squeezed' (castrated). Unfortunately, I did not get a chance to observe. This is what creates a 'wether'. I saw some of the young sheep limping around later in the day.

To work on the sheep like this, the entire population of the island's sheep must be rounded up. It can take half a day. The men and their dogs fan out over the island in a time-honoured pattern. The sheep gather in a flock naturally, the dogs dispatched after the stragglers. There is much shouting and shrill whistling. The natural boundary of the island shore is a help as the sheep are funnelled to the enclosure at the slip. There they are penned and individually pass along a narrow gangway where they can be observed, attended to, sheared, dipped, injected, wormed, marked or whatever else is required. Then they are released.

The sheep men had to go to the cliffs on the far side of the island, back at the lighthouse, to rescue some sheep. I offered to go around by sea in the punt with them but it turned out to be unnecessary.

Thought for the day: it would be a lonely place here without the sheep.

Got sore throat/cold again. Irritating.

Thursday, October 7

Head cold, sore throat, continues unabated. I sure hope I build up some immunity to them. Up late as a consequence but got much done. Especially, I got a bookshelf built out of boxes, old drawers and driftwood to take all the books I am unloading from *Molly B.* It almost looks like a classic piece of Scandinavian designer furniture.

At low tide I went over to the rocky beach to collect a lock of limpets. In the evening I attempt to turn them into limpet chowder. It doesn't look very appetizing.

Limpets are the pyramid-shaped sea clams which can be found on the rocks on any shore in Ireland. They are easy to dislodge with a hammer or any sharp weapon. The heel of your boot will do nicely. The tide does not have to be out very far either. In a few minutes of

foraging, enough food for a meal is easily obtained. An instant and unlimited source of food. The only problem is they are a bit tough. I ate them at least once a week and never really figured out what was the best way to cook them.

Tomas O'Crohan, the famous 'Blasket Islandman', mentions foraging for limpets.

Friday, October 8

Up to Pattens in the punt on the tide for shopping and post. There is a handy landing spot below the pub on the sound. It is sometimes used as a site for yawl races.

The calm sunny day brought a gallery of onlookers out from the pub to see the island man doing his thing. Most of them were fishermen having a pint. Some fishermen have been arrested in the Celtic

Sea while protesting a herring closure, and that was all the buzz up at the pub.

I motored back on the ebb tide and had a try at mackerel fishing out as far as the Lighthouse Steps. No luck.

I noticed an unusual thing on the rocky shore of Achillbeg. A wrecked currach. It had been there a few days and nobody bothers with it. I salvaged it by attaching a line and towing it to the slip about half a mile away. It's certainly beyond repair – a flabby slab of canvas laths and tar – but I have a plan to use it to cover my supply of turf.

Back up at the house, and since it was still dry and calm I got into a big window painting spree. The windows were bare wood and they really needed a bit of protection. I did the back window, the front west window and the two porch windows. A good afternoon's effort.

Saturday, October 9

Weather still calm but light rain. Rushed at the windows with second coat and they were dry enough by evening to install one.

A big team of islanders came in for a sheep roundup. I went over to the slip to have a look. The lambs were being injected, getting a shot of 'dose' in the mouth, being marked with a dye and having their tail snipped off in one efficient operation. The tail is whipped off with a knife and the lambs don't appear to feel much pain. This tail snipping is done to keep them clean. One of the sheep men asked me if I stayed on the island at night? I said, 'yes I did.' I think he was trying to make some point.

I said hello to a woman who was there looking on. She was well wrapped up in a huge tweed coat. She owns some of the sheep. She was nice and friendly to me. She said she had gone to school here on the island.

Painting and carving into the night.

Sunday, October 10

Big cleanup at house after breakfast then spent the day unloading and sorting gear from the *Molly B* at the slip. Martin Kilbane (brother to Pádraig Kilbane) and his wife and seven beautiful kids, all red-haired, came by and inspected the *Molly B*. Martin described how his trawler had broken loose in 120 miles per hour winds the previous winter. She had been tied to the pier at Cloghmore. He thought the pier might break away, the wind was so strong. His boat broke her lines at the pier and ran ashore at the entrance to the sound at Darby's Point. He grabbed a line from her as she went by and 'took a turn' around the boat house. 'She did £3,000 worth of damage to the keel. Fishing has been bad these last three years. You cannot sell a boat,' he said.

He is planning to go fishing for oysters from a currach with a six horsepower outboard which he is about to buy. It's for the Christmas trade on the natural oyster beds near Westport. Two men can make £350 a day between them. It seems silly to me but all the owners of 50-foot fishing boats are laying them up and going fishing in currachs.

Monday, October 11

It's a misty, calm day. Down to the slip at midday to catch the top of the tide and over to Cloghmore to haul off the last of my load of turf in the punt. It was about half a boat load. That makes five and a half boat loads in all I have shipped over to the island. And just as well I had no more. It's a lot of work shipping it across, unloading it and stacking it securely. Not to mention the job of then hauling it up to the house. I clean out the punt, the bilges of which are covered in turf dust. Now, let winter begin.

I spoke to old Mrs. Kilbane at the pier. She said she had cut turf as a little girl on Achillbeg. There are a couple of places on the island where a shallow bog exists. She said she thought I had been sold a 'soft load'. I said I was quite happy with it.

Tuesday, October 12

I got the midnight weather forecast last night which promised gales. At 5.00 a.m. it started to blow hard. I went down to the slip in the morning and secured a few things. The wind eased off towards mid-day though barometer was falling all day and is presently 988 having fallen 0.2 in the last two hours. I think this might be the lowest I have ever recorded it. I took the barometer off *Molly B*. It's a bit of an obsession – checking the barometer. It's what happens if one reads too many voyaging books and listens to too many shipping forecasts.

I am hoping to get away to Dublin in the morning. I tripped the punt off quite far at the slip so that it will be floating in the morning. The times of the tide are against me.

'Tripping a punt' is a technique for keeping the punt off a beach while the tide comes and goes. I use it constantly on Achillbeg where the rise and fall of tide can be up to 18 feet or more. A light anchor

is balanced on the bow of the punt and the punt is pushed out into deep water. A line is attached to the anchor and when the punt is in position the line is pulled or 'tripped'. The anchor falls into the water and the punt is then, hopefully, anchored in deep water independent of the state of the tide. The trip line, leading to the shore, is secured above the high water mark. When one wants to use the punt, the rope, or trip line, attached to the anchor is pulled and the punt comes onto the beach. 'Tripping' a boat requires a bit of practice. It is not always feasible and is highly dependent on prevailing conditions, such as the wind direction or current.

I did some tidying up at the house prior to leaving.

A bad leak through the roof in the center of the main room has appeared. Will have to do something about that.

Chapter 5

The West's Awake

But look! A voice like thunder spake,
The West's awake! The West's awake!
– Thomas Davis

Monday, October 18

A trip up to the capital. The trick about going up to Dublin is to try to get out as fast as possible and back to one's island fortress. Like that famous Kerry footballer, Mick O'Connell, who had to get back to his island home on Valentia after a game. Before he became contaminated by the big city.

I didn't do so badly this time round. Departed Wednesday at about 10.00 a.m. Late start – I missed the earlier bus from Achill Sound which would have allowed me some time in Castlebar before boarding the 11.30 train to Dublin.

On dropping the outboard in Pádraig's house above the pier I got a cup of tea, a piece of apple pie and a lift to the bus with Joe the German who works on the fishing boats. Joe speaks English with a great German/Achill accent. I had been prepared to walk the three miles to the sound if necessary. I tied the boat up to a piece of iron scrap on the slipway and left her so that if she filled I would not lose the oars or row locks. In the event she was fine and safe.

Bus from Achill Sound to Westport, train to Dublin. Only a half hour delay as they announced that the 'signal's broken down' at Portarlington.

Spent the next few days running around Dublin, meeting old friends and spending all my money on art materials.

I stayed with my Dad. I am sure he worried about his son who insisted he was an Irish version of Andy Warhol. Not only that, his son wanted to live on an uninhabited island off the west coast of Ireland with no apparent means of financial support. That is when he was not attempting to be an Irish version of Sir Francis Chichester or Eric Taberly!

The Westport train line was famous in those days for breakdowns, delays and also the price of the sandwiches and tea served on board. Many a caller to Gay Byrne would complain about the watery tea served in paper cups and the price charged.

To return to my island fortress I caught the Monday train for Westport. There was a half hour delay at Claremorris. The train coming in the opposite direction had 'broken down and was blocking the way'. That was the announcement. I got off the train in Castlebar to try to regain some pictures from the Song Contest Exhibition. I had not won a prize. I caught the bus to Achill Sound at 5.45 p.m.

There was good craic on the bus as two lads got on. I think that they might have come out of the Central Mental Hospital in Castlebar. They installed themselves in the back seat and started singing songs with a nice game young lass who had a good voice. She sang one very beautiful song and had the bus in the palm of her hand as we all listened. She also managed to keep the lads in rein when they started to sing anything bawdy. 'Arrah, I don't like those type,' she said. The bus wound its way on the rocky, dark wet road through Newport and Mulranny while we all listened enthralled to Moore's famous melodies.

The enchanting young singer gets off at my stop when we arrived at the turn off for Cloghmore. It is dark. I scurry on ahead of her on the road. She catches up, having been picked up by a car which was waiting to collect her. I stuck out my thumb. The car stopped. It was driven by her mother. I had done a lot of hitchhiking, including a thumbing trip from Istanbul to Dublin. It was rare, nearly unknown, to be picked up by a female driver, especially at night.

Before I got into the car, the female driver asked me if I had friends at Cloghmore. I said I had many. I stayed silent as we drove along at 15 miles per hour. I then explained I was staying on the island of Achillbeg and the woman said that she was born there and now lived over on the Atlantic Drive. So she probably knew who I was to start with. She mentioned the disaster, the drowning of the islander crossing. She kept telling me to be careful on the crossing. We bemoaned the declining population. Apparently at Bunacurry it is up but in this area down, the measurement being school attendance. Also, there is some industry at Bunacurry. The daughter stayed conspicuously silent all this time. She certainly did not sing any songs! The mother explained that normally she would not pick up people on the road. I said I understood. As I headed off into the night I said, 'God Bless'.

The tide was high. The punt was in fine shape, floating, water below the floor board level, ready to go. It had been a windy weekend all over the country.

Over at the slip on the island, *Molly B* was showing signs of the rough weather. The hull was held in position on the beach by seven lines. One of them, at the bow, I had tied too tight and it had frayed through. The strain had then come on the two-inch hemp line and the knot where it joined some nylon had come undone. The strain was then taken up by the three-inch poly line which was from a ring firmly anchored in cement on shore to the bowsprit waterline fitting. *Molly B* had moved down the beach a bit I think. I hope the keel is not too worn. All in all, *Molly B* is a bit of a worry where she is berthed.

I trudge up the track to the house carrying what I can. I had to get into the house by the window as the door lock had jammed. The lock seizes up regularly in the damp, salty, rain-driven atmosphere. I will sort out the lock in the morning. On with the kettle and light the fire. Home sweet home. Door to door, Dublin to Achillbeg Island, has taken about eleven and a half hours. Car, train, pause, train, bus, lucky hitchhike, boat and foot. Not bad.

Tuesday, October 19

Reasonably busy day with a hint of the 'back from the city' blues, 'what's it all about' and all that.

At about 9.00 in the morning I saw the fox down by the slip rummaging about in the seaweed at high water mark. The fox saw me as I came along and took off up the hill. I didn't do a thorough investigation of what the fox was rummaging at, for fear of disturbing it, and could not see what it was eating. Maybe it's a she fox and I wonder if it's alone. I'm reading the collected weekly columns of Michael Viney from *The Irish Times* in book form at present and he seems to confirm that foxes do scavenge on the shore line a lot. Viney

had recently taken up residence on the other side of Clew Bay from where he submitted his weekly column to the *Times*, called 'Another Life'. Though I never met him, I sort of identified with him and his concerns. Homesteading, the local fauna and flora and customs of the people. He was way ahead of me in terms of knowledge and experience. But I felt a kinship with Viney and his wife Ethna across the bay. He is still there, writing away in his weekly column, I am impressed to report.

I brought up to the house from the slip two knapsack loads of turf. This method of turf transportation rather than the wheelbarrow is the business. It feels more human, walking along, singing 'a knapsack on my back. . . I love to go a wandering.' I also can use a walking stick. Using the wheelbarrow makes me feel a bit like a beast of burden. But with a knapsack and stick it's more like taking a walk. But each trip is less turf transported. I have to do the mile-long trip to the slip twice a day to keep the insatiable fire burning.

Molly B is a bit of a workboat, beached as she is at the top of the tide. A yacht should be tied up in a marina, but you can abuse a workboat. Like the Swiss Family Robinson or the Bounty Mutineers at Pitcairn I was stripping my boat and using the contents to build a home on the island. Food, tools, books, utensils, blankets and clothes all made the long trek up to the house in stages. As the tides move into neaps, the hull remains grounded solidly on the steep, stony beach to which it is tethered. The mutineers on Pitcairn are reputed to have destroyed their ship, the *Bounty*, when they had landed everything. Burning their boat certainly made their decision to stay final. I had no intention of doing that.

It's a blustery mild day with some rain. All systems are go with the art work in the house. Also spent a couple of hours making a colour chart with all my new Windsor and Newton watercolours bought on the recent trip to Dublin. I now have all the colours in the range, for what that is worth. It's the opposite of the advice in the books, which tell one to limit one's palette as much as possible.

It was an expensive thing to do, to get the full range at a time when I did not have much money. But it was a sort of statement. I had to figure it out for myself. Some tubes cost over £4.00 each. Total cost around £200 for the full range. Proper watercolour brushes are very expensive also. They are supposed to be Kolinski sable. I once bought a watercolour brush for £80.00. It was no better than synthetic ones costing £10.00.

Thursday, October 21

A couple of days' work, and time seems to be flying. I started making a 'currach in a milk bottle' as a 'craft industry product for the west'. A craft industry doomed to failure. I am timing myself doing it and so far, with a whittled currach and a bottle on its stand, I have spent at least two hours. A dolphin in a jam jar comes next. One tries to imagine a product for the west which is craft- or souvenir-related, but in vain. Carved walking sticks might be a possibility, but I imagine that product is well catered for. I had plans for a big illustrated map of Clew Bay with all its islands which would have been a good one for gift shops, but I never got around to it.

Don't know whether to fill the currach in the milk bottle with turf or not. And am also planning a seagull outboard with two passengers. Then, whittling away on one of the passengers I lopped off his head and cut myself. So much for that – time to do something sensible.

Everybody who comes to the west with good intentions (as I have) to improve the place is doomed to failure. Start an industry, open a hotel, establish a religion, farm lobsters, raise alpacas, find gold. It's all been tried and all failed. There is no reason the arts should be any different. The west has a habit of just enduring. You cannot change it. You cannot improve it.

I am sleeping in the main room now, on the sofa, in front of the smoldering fire. I did not have the energy to move back into the back room since returning from Dublin. It is too grotty, too damp and too

close to the wind- and rain-battered west end gable of the house. I think I can feel another sore throat coming on.

I am living on coffee brewed on the turf fire. Produces a tangy, turf-scented brew with a faint hint of ash dust and an opaque sepia colour. Would be a big hit in the cafés of New York.

Looking forward to tomorrow's sally out to the post office and to Achill Sound in the punt, weather permitting.

Friday, October 22

Spent a cold night last night, on the borders of hypothermia. I should not complain. It's my decision to stay here. And it's going to get a lot colder. I simply have to get my bedding better organised.

Up early and motored in the punt up to Achill Sound. It's a nice day. A 'soft' day, mild, misty, rainy. Light southwest winds. The distance is about two miles and the expedition has to be planned with military precision. That is, one has to know the time of the high tide!

I leave the slip at about two hours before the top of the tide and thus am able to use the flooding tide and deep water to ride the current all the way to Achill Sound. It's a wonderful, scenic excursion. To starboard is the brooding sepia bulk of Corraun Hill. To port, the lower lying, coastal strip of Achill Island with the road running close to the shoreline. On both sides are the clusters of cottages with their smoking chimneys. It's like sailing through a Paul Henry painting. The sky, the hills, the cottages. The purple layers of backdrop.

The water is shallow in places. The channel meanders from side to side but is always obvious, marked at the side by exposed reefs or tufts of floating seaweed. The pilotage is interesting but not demanding in the shallow draft punt.

The tide swishes me in past the old coastguard station at Darby's Point, past the moored boats in the anchorage, close to the famous tower house of Granuaile at Kildavnet, past the cemetery where tourists stop, then on up to the church, school and pub at Dereens. Cars stop on the road to see the unusual sight of a boat in the sound in October. On past the bay at Bleanaskill. Then Sraheens with its abandoned cottages down on the shore line and then the amazing growth of rhododendrons near the sound. Past the church ruin on the Corraun side and finally into the large shallow basin close to the swing bridge. This is where the two tide streams meet. One flowing down from Bulls Mouth to the north, the other bringing me up from the south, starting at Darby's Point.

I tie up to the causeway which carries the road out to the swing bridge. The bridge has not swung in many years. Like a lot of things around here it needs a little lubrication. It's a short hop and a skip across the road to Sweeney's, purveyors of everything a man could want.

I have at least an hour before the tide turns and starts running south again with the ebb.

I had a big shopping spree in the shops at the sound. Money is running low. I have got less than £10 cash now it would seem. But I am well stocked up on most items. I got some petrol for the outboard at the nice service station at the sound.

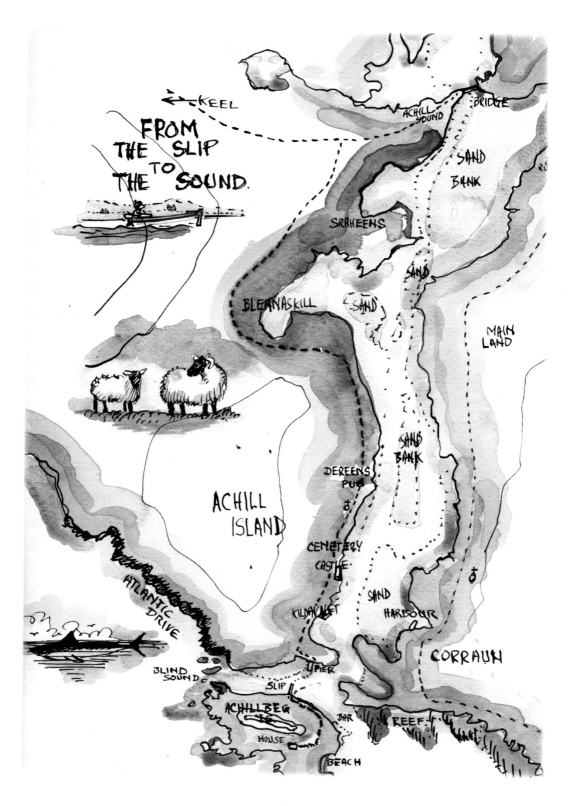

I set off back down the sound as the tide turns. I can ignore the channel because the tide is full. I stop and explore an abandoned cottage here and there at the water's edge. People prefer to live close to the road. There is the wreck of an ancient steamer in the middle of the sound. Trapped in the sand, evidence of its boiler and ribs still defying the current. Large clumps of seaweed grow like trees on the sandbanks and have to be avoided lest they foul the prop of the outboard. In the old days the seaweed was harvested and used as a fertilizer. There are photos of islanders floating across the sound on large rafts of harvested seaweed.

I stop at Dereens on the way back, walking up to the road through the fields. At the post office I get a letter from Georganna Maloff, my old carving mentor from Vancouver. She is threatening to visit me on my island. She seems to think there is a thriving artist's colony here. Maybe I have misled her in one of my effusive letters ...

As the punt was exiting the sound at Darby's Point I espied an otter. This is the first time I have ever seen one in the wild. It surfaced quite near the boat. For a brief instant I was staring straight at it and it was staring back at me, our eyes locked. At first I thought it was a seal but it was much smaller. It was munching away on something and showed its white fangs and yellow mouth the way I have never seen a seal do. It also has a lumpier, more angular head and I could clearly see its long whiskers and furry face. Then with a flick of its tail it was gone. I stopped the motor and waited for a while but no luck. It didn't reappear as a seal would have. Otters are very shy creatures.

Saturday, October 23

Quite a productive day, mainly painting. Big step forward as I scrap my palette of over nearly two years and adopt one recommended from a Windsor and Newton pamphlet. My old one had been completely disorganised. I made a colour chart and got outside

to do a sketch of Cloghmore and try out some recommended colour mixes.

I do some letter writing, including a letter to Georganna in far off Canada. I have a bath, and do some laundry in the bath.

Sunday, October 24

Over to Cloghmore in the punt. I was half way to the Dereens church on foot when I realised I was an hour late for Mass. The clocks had changed. It's winter time. I sat for a few minutes in the church contemplating my existence. In a place where there is universal peace and quiet, the splendour and majesty of nature, why does one need to go to a church for contemplation?

I headed back to my island.

I'm getting into a routine. Sunday, it's house clean-up day. I take everything out of the main room. All the furniture, carpets and tools go outside the front door. Big sweep out. Carpets and rugs, such as they are, go outside and get a thrashing with a broom. The floor of the house is raw, crumbly concrete. The week's supply of ash from the fire place goes flying in a bucket down the hill to fertilise the fields in a cloud of dusty smoke. I sweep out the main room and return all the furniture again. The kitchen/bathroom gets a going over. Sand, dust, cobwebs, woodlice, nice big beetles, fruit flies, earwigs, daddy longlegs, all go scurrying. Luckily, no rats or mice. Cleanliness is next to godliness. Got a lot of discipline around here. I feel like Captain Bligh and Fletcher Christian all rolled into one.

That done and the house put back together again, maybe it's time for a bit of brunch. Then a free afternoon. A walk to the lighthouse, to the fort or maybe take a trip over to Corraun. Something for a change. The routine helps to regulate the passing of time.

Monday, October 25

Today is a bank holiday elsewhere, I do believe, but here on Achillbeg it's business as usual. We work.

When I decided to be an artist it took a certain amount of thinking and, in the end, self-belief. For a while I rushed around asking people, usually other artists, if they thought it was a good idea. Most of them were skeptical, telling me that it would be difficult to make a living as an artist. They always honed in on the money. I got relatively little encouragement in the Dublin of the early 1970s.

Among the people I did ask and who are, today, well known, was Bruce Arnold, who I happened to meet at the time. He gave what was possibly the best answer. 'Well,' he said, 'what will you do if you don't become an artist?' He then backed it up by buying some work from me.

Mild calm day with wind from the east and barometer very high. (1010). In the evening the wind increased and it started to rain.

I saw the fox. It darted out of an abandoned house as I walked by. It has a lot of grey hairs mixed in with the red in its tail. Maybe it is a sign of age and anxiety? And one cannot really blame it I suppose. There are a few people about here who would gladly put a bullet through its red furry head. It's a tough, hard life being a sheep farmer. It cannot be easy eking out an existence as a fox on a western island either. Sometimes I feel that I am caught a bit in between.

Tuesday, October 26

Having started to blow yesterday evening the wind built up over the night until it was a full gale. Blowing stink. I could not sleep with the noise of rattling slates and windows. Outside was pitch black. I could have been on the far side of the moon. I lay in a half sleep, half dreaming state and looking at the ceiling which sounded as if it would fly off into the sea at any moment. Slowly the dawn came up. The sheep outside were huddled against the sheltered side of walls. The fields were covered with white spume from the crashing waves.

I wrapped up well and flew downwind to the slip to check on things. It was a scene of mayhem. The currach wreck had been blown off the turf pile which it was sheltering, even though it had been weighted down with rocks. The punt had sunk on its mooring and was floating awash, full of water. This is the first time I have seen this happen. It might have got fouled beneath one of the lines holding *Molly B*. I pulled the punt in as best I could but could not get the anchor to come in. So I removed the oars and left it to dry out. Luckily, the motor was not on the punt overnight but was up above the high water mark in the shelter of a wall.

I struggled back against the wind to the house. I had a look around. The cover had blown off the fresh water tank located on a hill behind the house. This was heavy, plywood and felt slab, weighted down with stones. Another first. The downpipe from the gutters on the back of the house had been blown off the wall. This probably means that this is the strongest it has blown all year. It's still blowing now. Watching the barometer all day it fell a bit but stayed high and presently is up there at 1015. So there must be reasons, other than a low barometer, causing the blow. Or maybe it will get worse.

There is a rawness and a power to the wind. The stone walls and the tufted grass are the only elements which can survive. That's why there are no trees. The sheep take shelter in the lee of the walls. They cannot graze. The lambs are confused and startled and run about aimlessly unable to feed. The waves crash against the cliffs on the west side of the island. They bounce back to battle the oncoming waves stirring up a tattered, spume-topped maelstrom. On the sheltered side of the island, the bar, right across from Achillbeg to the rocky flats at Corraun is a confused mess of white water where the swell breaks. The sky looks the colour and weight of lead.

When the tide is at its lowest I returned to the punt at the slip and bailed it out. I retied the lines. The tides are in neap so luckily *Molly B* is not affected, being high and dry on the shale bank. The tender to *Molly B*, a 9-foot fiberglass dinghy, was also moved by the wind but was saved by its lines.

I've done what I can do for my fleet of boats. Back at the house I wrote a couple of pages of the first draft of the book which became many years later *The Log of the Molly B*. I spend a lot of time looking out the window at the mayhem outside.

Wednesday, October 27

I seem to be developing a routine to my working day, just as I have for Sunday. First thing some writing, then breakfast, some artwork of some sort, then down to the slip to check on boats and collect load of turf in the knapsack. I am using the abandoned house nearby as a location to stockpile a supply of turf. At the same time it keeps it dry. It makes a huge difference to the flammability of turf if it has a chance to dry out a bit. Lunch, and then I drift into the afternoon, which is less structured. It tends to depend on the weather and if I can do something outside or not.

I did some major house work today, a small job which grew. I noticed a huge draught coming from the attic above the kitchen, making the east bedroom like a wind tunnel. As the weather becomes colder the draughts become very noticeable. This was because two of the wooden slats nailed to the rafters had been removed when the house was wired for electricity. The slats had not been replaced and now let in a lot of wind. They are in a sort of attic storage area. I plug as many of the holes in the slats with heavy duty industrial plastic bags of which there seems to be a limitless supply knocking about.

The roof is like a threadbare jumper. When the wind gets up and the slates rattle, the wind rushes in. There is nothing to impede it. There are many gaps between the laths of wood, which is the next and final line of defense. If only they had been into insulation and global warming in 1935. But then they had their thatch. Most of the houses would have been thatched prior to the building of the one I was in. Thatch would have been a good insulation against the wind and the thatched houses would have been smaller and lower and therefor easier to heat with the smoldering turf. When I am a Famous Artist Living on an Island I will pay someone to insulate this place.

Speaking of money, looking forward to Friday and shopping. I went through all of my pockets and came up with £8.00 – my worldly wealth.

The wind moderated much today.

Thursday, October 28

Another slow day, the doldrums perhaps. Looking at my watch, looking at my calendar, reading Viney, sitting in front of the fire, looking out the windows.

But in fact got quite a bit done. Some painting – outdoor in the mild, dry, windy weather. I painted a view of Corraun and Cloghmore and indoors started a big painting of a radar reflector.

I did pictures of radar reflectors for a while. A series, I suppose. The subject had several advantages. 1) The complex planes of the metal reflector were almost abstract, yet had an interesting shape. 2) The arcane meaning of the subject was only known to a select few who knew marine equipment. 3) The geometric shapes of the reflector were reminiscent of cubism, a style which I have always liked. 4) They were, in a roundabout way, marine paintings. 5) There was a visual pun based around the title, 'reflector'. 6) The radar reflector was an important piece of safety equipment for the single-hander, therefore the paintings had an ironic reading.

But radar reflector paintings did not really catch on. Maybe I was wrong to do so, but I searched about for a subject about which I could

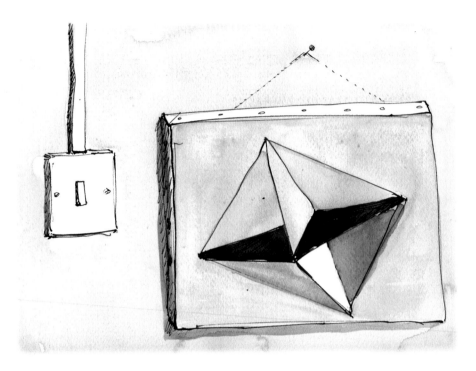

become obsessive. There have been a few recurring themes over the years – boxes, bicycles, boats being perhaps the most persistent.

A big reshuffle in the workshop, hauling all the lumber out to the main room, moving furniture about and stashing chairs in the abandoned house next door. The house next door is proving a handy storage facility.

The fox got christened. I saw it for a long stint as it rummaged in the fields in front of the house, unaware that it was being observed. It must eat insects or mice or something with his long snout. It has a lot of grey on either side of its back and tail. Still not sure of the sex. Keeps his tail low down between his legs! The name? Slim Pickings.

Found on the rocky beach a fine piece of driftwood, a five-foot long piece of birch log. About six to eight inches in diameter. I lugged it up to the house. Planning to try to build a carving easel with it.

Friday, October 29

It was a blustery morning and I thought it might be difficult to get out for the weekly trip to the shop and post office. But it eased off by afternoon and by top of the tide was calm and mild.

The punt at the slip was full of water again. It's difficult to say how it happens. Maybe the wind blowing against the outgoing tide builds up such a steep sea that the punt sticks its bow under and so fills with water. It shows how powerful the wind can be as the anchorage is sheltered. A life jacket stored in the bow was on the beach. Luckily, it had not blown away. The oars were safe. I baled out the punt and, practicing prudence these days, motored over to the pier and walked the mile to the post office at Dereens. The mail was a statement from the Bank of British Columbia saying I had 77 Canadian dollars. In Vancouver. Lucky me. Somehow I'll have to get my hands on it.

I stopped in at the overgrown graveyard at Kildavnet looking for treasures in the stone carving vein, which maybe I could use as inspiration for my own carving. It's a beautiful and evocative place. This is the graveyard where the remains of the victims of the drowning tragedy at Westport in 1894 are buried. Over thirty people died when their hooker capsized at Westport Quay. They were on their way to Scotland for the potato harvest. The first train to run on the newly built railway line brought the bodies home to Achill. The gravestones are simple and unadorned. Dark limestone with the local family names. The nearby monument of Granuaile's tower house is a fitting memorial.

Back at Cloghmore pier a JCB, a truck and four men were collecting a huge load of boulders from the beach to the west side of the pier. I should have asked them 'what for'. It gave me an idea. That was what I need on Achillbeg – a load of apprentices and some heavy duty tractors and cranes. We could build a causeway, a car park, a visitor's centre complete with art gallery. Studios and workshops. A sculpture garden. Then I could make some art work. I could collect all the erratic boulders on the island and string them into a giant spiral or latter day Stonehenge. Earthworks. A bit like my hero Claes Oldenburg who had proposed giant sculptures of everyday objects.

Actually, some thirty years later a disgruntled property developer/builder was to build a latter-day Stonehenge in Achill. A magnificent achievement, it was built in very short time using a battery of cranes, trucks and cement mixers. It is located close to the village of Keel.

And so by punt back to the slip. The tides are getting higher – coming into springs and *Molly B* will probably float at the top of the tide, around Sunday. I think it would be better to find a less exposed place for her for the winter.

Back up in the house I had a lengthy afternoon tea drinking session. Biscuits. The fire built up, the book I was reading was less than gripping. I dozed off on the sofa to wake at 2.00 a.m. the next morning to go to bed, properly.

Saturday, October 30

And I didn't get up that early either. A lie in. Perhaps in the great Irish tradition of 'taking to one's bed'.

The tides are in spring cycle. Went down to the slip to build a sea wall around the turf pile as a really high tide almost reaches the pile. I would not want the turf to float away. Windy from the east, mild, some rain.

Sunday, October 31

Rowed over to the pier at Cloghmore in the tender of the *Molly B*, the nine-foot dinghy. The tide was full out and the punt high and dry at the slip. When that happens it is a hard push down the beach to launch the heavy punt. Also, weather calm so easier to take the small boat.

It's a nice walk to and from Dereens.

Back at the house I had the now customary Sunday clean-up. Then I returned to the slip at the top of the tide where *Molly B* was floating once more. I released all the lines holding her in position and hauled in the anchors. *Molly B* slid out into deep water. Using the punt as a tug and the still flooding tide, I towed *Molly B* across to Cloghmore and inside the

shelter of the sound. Then, turning right, I headed over the sand banks to the little harbour of Corraun. There, I tied her up in the harbour where she will dry out each half tide. Inside, against the harbour wall, is a nice 35-foot double-ended half-decker. I think *Molly B* will be safer there when the wild wind blows. Far safer than where she was, beached at Achillbeg. In fact, Corraun might just be the safest harbour in Ireland.

I tidied up on board and set up the shore lines. As night and the tide fell I motored back over the sand banks to my island fortress. Back at the house by 8.30 p.m. That's *Molly B* settled for now, I hope. A good day's work and a relief!

Chapter 6

Feilimí's Little Boat and Feilimí in It

Báidín Fheilimí d'imigh go Gabhla,
Báidín Fheilimí is Feilimí ann.

Feilimí's little boat went to Gola,
Feilimí's little boat and Feilimí in it
– Traditional

Monday, November 1

Tried, at midday, to motor over to Corraun Harbour in the punt. The motor, a four-horsepower Evinrude, was not enough to push the punt against the ebb which was screaming out of the entrance to the sound. The tide runs through the narrows at Darby's Point at a good five knots when there are spring tides in a deep S-shaped river. There are spring tides now. It's a dramatic spot. There are back eddies and whirlpools and even mini-water spouts when the wind is high enough.

So I landed on the Corraun sandbanks on the mainland and walked the short distance through the dunes and fields to the harbour. Here on the sandbanks there is a colony of hundreds of rabbits. It's a nice walk. The rabbits scurry for their holes, *Watership Down*-fashion. Then it's across a few small fields and past ruined cottages to Corraun harbour. It's a route I take many times over the winter as the tide frequently prevents using the boat for the journey.

I did a much needed cleanup on the interior of *Molly B*, which was standing upright in the mud against the wall of the harbour. The half-decker, which had been parked inside, was gone.

I met the man who lives at the harbour. He has a nice, picture postcard perfect house. Like something out of *Beatrix Potter* and the Lake District rather than Ireland. He fishes for oysters in Westport. The oyster season has been good this year, or at least so he said, and it's unusual to hear 'good' from a fisherman. He has a bunch of kids in the picturesque little house at the harbour. They are taking a certain interest in my coming and going and in the *Molly B*.

I went back to Achillbeg for an afternoon of carving. I am making a chess set. I roughed out the pawns from the handles of old floor brushes. It's quite good wood for carving. Every pawn is to be different, each with a face. It is more whittling than carving as the pieces are so small.

'Whittling' is defined as carving where one hand holds the wood and the other hand holds the tool, whether it be knife or chisel. 'Carving' is where the wood is held in a vice or is free standing and the artist attacks it with a chisel and mallet. Well, that's my defini-

tion anyway. There is an interesting distinction between the carving which the Indians did in the Pacific Northwest, where I had just come from, and European carving. The Indians carved with adzes and axes. The European tradition of carving uses the mallet. In fact, the mallet is the most important tool in European carving. Thus the European carver always works away from himself using the mallet, whereas the indigenous artists carved towards themselves. Cutting 'away' from the body and using a mallet is much safer than pointing the chisel or adze at yourself, as any well trained carpenter will tell you. Academic art historians and anthropologists like to make these subtle distinctions.

The situation in Corraun harbour is not ideal. It looks as though *Molly B* will have to stay against the harbour wall. There is a lot of traffic across the deck and big trawlers come and go and tie up alongside. I am surprised there is so much traffic in the small, out of the way, harbour. *Molly B* becomes a huge fender. She rubs against the other boats on the outside and against the wall on the inside. Presumably, no one wants to be on the inside. Also, many rough, heavy lines, running in all directions, are rubbing on the cabin sides and the rail.

Tuesday, November 2

A sunny, calm day. Must be the full moon and the spring tides. I am working hard. I have lots of energy. The tides seem to be running in my veins. From my vantage point high on the island I can feel and see the energy of the cosmic forces pulling and pushing the water through the narrows, filling the shallows and coves. I sit on the hill of Achillbeg and look up to the north towards Achill Sound. I can see the whole universe in microcosm. Gaia. It's a pre-industrial landscape. Except for the field patterns it could be pre-historical. At low tide the land forming, the sand moving and filtering. Cleaning and renewing. At high tide the water surging against the limits of the land constricting and constraining it. Power. Always change, always

movement, conflict and calm. The sea and the tide feel like the blood running through my veins. I become one with the land, one with the cosmos, 'a piece of the continent, a part of the main'.

I espied a cargo ship heading out of Clew Bay, an unusual occurrence. Very few ships now enter the ports in Clew Bay, either Westport or Newport.

Once upon a time Westport was a busy destination and there was much seaborne traffic. It is a difficult harbour to enter. A pilot had to be picked up from the outlying islands to make the intricate passage to Westport Quay.

The family of W.B. and Jack Yeats had a mill in Westport Quay and it is still known as Pollexfen's Mill on the quay there. The family had a fleet of ships. When the Yeats family, living in London, wanted to return to Sligo they would go to Liverpool by train and board one of the family's ships. They would make the journey round the north coast of Ireland, stopping at various ports along the way.

The young Jack Yeats was inspired with a love of adventure, ships, pirates and characters by these trips.

I walked over to the lighthouse and watched the ship as it passed out of the bay. I painted a picture of Clare Island which ended up including the ship. Seems to be the same ship – red, 150 feet-long with a prominent deck crane, which anchored at Achillbeg about six weeks ago. Maybe they are carrying wood in from Scandinavia – latter day Vikings.

Went down to the slip to get a load of turf and I pick a lock of limpets on the way. Limpets really are an ideal food source. One can pick a supply as one takes a leisurely stroll with almost no effort. They are always there in abundance. Cooking them is fast and simple. They are a bit tough and chewy however. I threw them into a leftover spaghetti sauce and that seemed better than eating them on their own or in the chowder I tried the last time. The chowder was a lot of effort. I have yet to try currying them.

When I tell the local people I meet that I am eating limpets, or *bairneach* as they call them, they seem a bit shocked and amused. The eating of limpets is associated with the famine and a very bad time not so long ago. In Scotland they are more commonly accepted as a food source and appear in present day cookery books. Mesolithic middens are full of their shells. Apparently in Hawaii they are considered a delicacy. During the Great Famine, along with seaweed, they became the food of last resort. There are reports of them being eaten raw, something I find hard to believe. They are easy to cook – a few minutes in boiling water and they pop out of their shells ready to go. One of these days someone will discover them and they will become the new 'in' food.

I never did develop much of a taste for seaweed. Cooked or raw.

There is much action and excitement over at Cloghmore pier as the fishing fleet returns. Two of the modern pair trawlers have arrived. They are back from the south where they have been fighting the EEC regulations about herring fishing. And losing that battle.

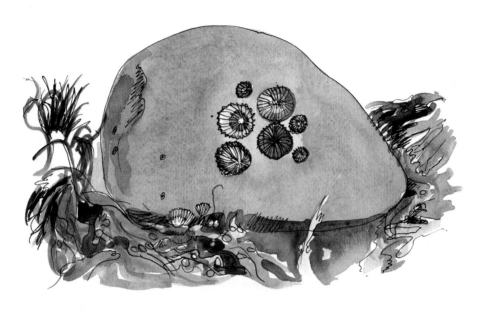

Some of the fishermen went to jail. At dusk the two big trawlers went out fishing for the night. They looked very well in the dim light on the calm sea of the bay, their powerful engines growling and deck lights twinkling. Like cruisers moving steadily out to do battle.

Pair trawling for herring is an exciting form of fishing. Like big game hunting. No patience or long hours are involved as in other forms of fishing. The herring come inshore and shoal at night. The trawler picks up a 'marking' on its sonar machine. A line is passed to the partner boat and the net 'shot' off its drum. Holding the big sock of a net open between the two boats and steering through the shoal with the aid of the sonar, the fish are scooped up in a single sweep. It is a skillful, risky business. The fish only shoal in shallow water at night and frequently near rocks. If the fishermen get it right they can fill the net and the fish hold of both boats in a matter of minutes. If they get it wrong they can lose gear worth thousands of pounds.

It's cold this evening so got a blazing fire going. I can see me wearing my down parka in the house before we are through.

Wednesday, November 3

The most famous artist associated with Achill is, of course, Paul Henry. He visited the island in 1910, loved it and stayed here pretty well until 1920. After that year, apparently, he never came back to Achill though he lived in Dublin for the rest of his life.

This period which he spent in Achill corresponds to the great upheavals in Europe. Paul Henry was having none of it. For the First Great War he and wife Grace painted away here in Achill. They exhibited in Belfast each year of the conflict to critical and, at times, commercial acclaim.

Henry was a sophisticated man who had lived in both Paris and London and associated with many educated people and artists. He had studied in Whistler's studio and formed his strong, simplified style there. He was sure when he arrived in the village of Keel on Achill Island that this was where he wanted to be. Like Joyce at much the same time, he was determined to find a uniquely Irish art. As he states in his memoir, he wanted to get 'the very soul of Ireland' into his work and decided that Achill was the best place to do that.

He had his wife Grace with him while he was in Achill, a thing he neglects to mention at all in his extensive and poetic memoir of living on the island. Perhaps this is because Grace was less enthusiastic about Achill than he was, and their marriage broke up during his stay on the island. They were estranged for the next twenty years but were able to maintain an artistic partnership, sharing a studio in Dublin and exhibiting together in Ireland and England for those years.

He apparently was offered a place to live on Achillbeg in an abandoned coastguard station, a building which no longer exists. It would have been a fantastic thing if he had done so and left a record. Instead he stayed in the Coastguard station at Cloghmore which is on Darby's Point at the south entrance to the sound (now demolished). So it is quite likely that he might have, at some stage, visited the island.

Paul Henry writes with great affection and understanding of the local people among whom he lived. It is curious that he never returned to visit the location of his early inspiration. He went on painting excursions to many other locations in the country over the years, and became the originator of a pastoral view of Ireland which became known all over the world.

He is particularly known for his treatment of the clouds, big masses of stratocumulus as they pile up over the bogs and sepia-tinted hills. It became a signature feature of his painting which he took with him when he left Achill and applied to many of his classic Irish landscape scenes. He never painted much outdoors. He had a meticulous, craftsman-like studio manner which would not have been appropriate to *en plein* air work. Presumably, he based his paintings on sketches done in the field.

Down at the slip I espied the Winkle Picker coming over for winkles. He rows across from Corraun in his currach, a considerable pull against the wind. Luckily, he can use the tide in both directions. He lands on the beach and then walks across the island to the rocky beach. Hours later, with his big sack of winkles on his back, he retraces his steps. It is hard work, I am sure. It's the spring tides, so best for foraging in the tidal pools on the west side of Achillbeg. Strange the effect of knowing I am not alone on the island. I am becoming territorial about my island home.

Thursday, November 4

An outdoor day. I started building a platform, a sort of patio, outside the front door of the house. The idea is to have a level area on which to work or sit outside. At present, the ground slopes away at quite an angle from the front of the house. The house is built on an irregular hill which has been landscaped into several attractive terraces over the years. These are in scrappy repair now, but you can discern how, over the years, they evolved. Here and there are the remains of older houses and sheds which would have been cannibalised for stones when building the newer structures.

To construct this patio I am moving a big pile of small stones, which 'is in an adjoining field, and dumping it outside the house. The stones have been assembled in the field, I presume, when the land was cleared. I do not disturb the walls or abandoned buildings. It's a bit like the sort of work which convicts do in the southern United States. Back on the chain gang.

In a fit of energy I cleaned all the sheep droppings out of the abandoned house next door as I am using it as a storage area. Then I boarded up the entrance.

It's a bit like a post-apocalyptic scenario here on the island. Or a post-modern landscape, a phrase which was then much in vogue. There is an unlimited supply of abandoned houses scattered about. If you need a new house you just choose one. Unfortunately, they are all empty and full of sheep droppings. If this was Hollywood they would be full of useful stuff like tinned food, stylish clothing and guns.

Friday, November 5

Grey day, still calm though. Some rain, some hazy sun. More routine: each morning I head over to the rocky beach to see if anything has come in on the tide and wind. It is always a buzz to head over to the rocky beach. Something unusual might have blown

up from the vast wastes of the Atlantic out there. There are the usual flotsam and jetsam, the buoys, bits of netting and smashed boxes from the fishing boats. Always, I am looking for firewood. Sometimes there will be a log that has come from Canada. Sometime a worm-eaten baulk from a pier in Florida. Bits of rope are welcome, what I once heard a local calling 'Spanish twine'. It is always polypropylene rope because it floats. Bright blue, red and green. Very occasionally it might be something unusual, a boat wreck or piece of equipment. Maybe something valuable ...

This morning, instead of my usual walk to the rocky beach, I do some rock moving from the fields in front of the house to supply the material for the patio. After about a week of this I should have a sufficient supply for the platform. I don't know yet if I will have to use gravel and sand to cement it all in place.

Whittling on a chess set. King and queen and couple of rooks. The rooks don't seem great but rooks are difficult. I'm trying to line up Fanny, the horse, for a drawing session to model for the knight. The castle design will be easy. That has to be based on Granuaile's tower house nearby.

It got dark very early today but it's going to get worse before we are through this winter.

Big break with routine today. I did not get my Friday run out to the post office at Dereens. This is pretty well because I have no cash and did not want to go just for post. Pattens shop has offered me credit but I do not want to take it, at least not until things get worse. There is plenty of food in the house. I miss the odd loaf of bread though and the whole ritual of having to make the trip. I also like to get out on Friday on the remote chance there might be a message from somebody coming to visit for the weekend.

With this in mind I walked down to the slip at 10.30 p.m. and picked up a load of turf. There was a wonderful full moon, no wind and I could not sleep. It would be a long, outside chance to arrive there at the slip when someone arrived at Cloghmore pier looking to get across to the island. I gazed across at the glittering pier lights and the resting fishing boats reflected on the water. All was quiet. I walked back up along the track gazing out over the shimmering silver of Clew Bay and the outline of Croagh Patrick across the bay. The bright grey stone walls, the dark bulk of the houses, the startled sheep scurrying out of my way. The clear crescent of the beach and the waves gently breaking on it. A Wordsworth moment. Perhaps I'm lonely.

Saturday, November 6

Rereading the above: 'Yerra musha a vic. Will ya grab a hold of yourself.'

I met the lighthouse man. He comes over to Achillbeg frequently to tend the lighthouse. He tells me that *Molly B* seemed safe and sound over in Corraun near where he lives. It's good that someone is keeping an eye on her.

Whittling knights. Went and did drawing of Fanny, the white horse who lives alone on the island, her only companion a goat. She is a Connemara pony. Fanny and the goat hang around together as buddies amid the anonymous scattering of 500 sheep, something which is most amusing to observe. Fanny refused some turnip peels which I brought to her. Picky eater.

I'm eating up a supply of old tinned baby food I found in the house which must have been here quite some time. Cannot imagine who the baby was. It's delicious – stewed fruit, which I put on pancakes.

Cold today, noticeably so last night in bed. The barometer has been falling all this sunny day. This evening it's blowing a bit and raining.

Sunday, November 7

The barometer is down and it's windy from the east south east. There is nothing much happening. Sam Beckett should try coming here. I tried reading his novel *Molloy* but found it heavy going. Ironically, with its character in bed dressed in shabby overcoats and

with nothing much happening most of the time, there are comparisons with this winter, west of Ireland scene. Maybe I am becoming a Beckett character. *Molloy* is, of course, the novel in which the famous sucking stones passage takes place. Achillbeg would be ideal for such a dialogue, there being no shortage of suitable sucking stones on the rocky beach. You cannot suck just any stone but a stone which has been shaped, rounded and cleaned by the eternal cosmic movement of the tides is ideal. If nothing happens 'twice' in his famous *Waiting for Godot*, then nothing happens a lot more often here. Beckett preferred exile in Montparnasse rather than the west of Ireland. There he creates an imaginary world in much of his work which is hard to identify. I see that world all about me here. The coffee in Montparnasse would be a lot better but it would not have that faint hint of turf smoke.

I'll go on. I went over to Corraun around midday to light a fire in the boat stove, check on things and have a spot of lunch there. Boat interior undisturbed, though I forgot to lock the companionway. Some onlookers came down the pier and hung about while I worked on the boat. They spoke in Irish. Corraun is a strong Gaeltacht area.

Back to house for a clean-up. Then disaster strikes. I broke a tooth on a piece of bone in a lamb chop. This seems serious and I may have to go and find a dentist.

Monday, November 8

Up later than usual (9.00 a.m.) to rainy, misty day. Wind back in the west but not strong. Reading up on Irish art, Bruce Arnold's *Concise History of Irish Art*, the well-known Thames and Hudson tome.

The other famous artist associated with Achill is Alexander Williams (1846–1930) who lived near Achillbeg in a house which he built and tended for many years at Bleanaskill. This is about half way between Achillbeg and Achill Sound. He established a fine garden at Bleanaskill which is still there. He came to Achill in 1899 and was there, and well known, when Paul Henry arrived in 1910. They do not seem to have had much contact. This is surprising in that they were both from similar Anglo Protestant backgrounds. In addition, both exhibited at the same time in the RHA annual shows in Dublin.

In his book about Achill, Paul Henry likes to stake his claim that Achill was his artistic discovery. In fact, Alexander Williams (and others) had been painting the people, the landscape and the seascape of Achill long before Henry arrived.

Paul Henry's training in Paris and London was much more so-phisticated than the almost self-taught, enthusiastic amateur Williams. The years have been kind to the reputation of Paul Henry, less so in the case of Alexander Williams. It is almost the story of the ascendancy of modernism (represented by Henry) over academi-cism (represented by the traditional Williams).

Henry writes about the common people on Achill. He befriended the outcasts and characters. He drank quite a bit. Williams was more at home having tea in the drawing rooms of the landlords and the church-going gentry. Williams was a favorite of the Castle set in Dublin. Henry, while remarkably apolitical, had many friends of a nationalist leaning. Perhaps this is what separated them.

I am making a clothes rack for over the bath to allow washed clothes to drip dry into the bath. And a similar arrangement for in front of the fire. Which may sound a bit serious and mundane, but that is what it has come down to. Domestic chores. When I am a Famous Artist Living on an Island I can get one of the apprentices to do these uncreative chores as a sort of initiation.

I seem to be burning about a knapsack full of turf per day. That's if the fire smolders through the morning, but it uses more if it is blaz-ing away. The weather is getting perceptibly colder.

Tuesday, November 9

Doing some dry stone wall building as I build up the sides of the patio. I don't know if I should use cement or not, and if I do, whether to use it on the side retaining walls or just for the top surface. Would seem that to use on the top only would be stupid as the structure would be sure to settle. Looks like I might have to do some gravel hauling. Stone structure building around here is a subtle art.

Cold. Wind builds up over day to gale force at present. Time dragging to the extent that I have to force myself to put in the hours in the workroom and stay away from the fireside seat where I am reading art books.

Any art books I can get my hands on that is. They are a scarce commodity around here. Bruce Arnold's *History of Irish Art* I am going through slowly. According to Arnold, 'John Henry Foley, 1818–1874, is the most important sculptor Ireland has ever produced'. So there. I think I'd give it to Seamus Murphy.

Wednesday, November 10

Somewhat of a slow day. I get down to the slip early (8.30) as the wind howled all night, rattling the windows and roof, keeping me awake. The punt is OK but had dragged its anchor about ten yards. I put a better line on to it from the rings on the slip and returned at 1.00 p.m. at top of the tide to adjust the line.

Heavy hail and wind all day, and thunder. In a bad mood generally. Bed for an hour in the afternoon. At 5.00 p.m. the lights go out for two hours as the electricity fails. Cold and did not get much work done in workroom.

Thursday, November 11

Hacked into some production frame making, churning out three at once. That way I can concentrate on the process efficiencies. For example, I save a piece of wood by designing the frame to fit the many 34-inch long slats I have. Vincent gave me a huge collection of teak slats which he had intended to make into lobster pots. He never got around to it and the slats lay for years in a garage. Then plastic lobster pots came along.

Vincent started a salmon smoking business in Westport and used to go all over north Mayo buying fish for his business. Once he met Eric Clapton who had come to Mayo to pursue one of his passions, which is fishing. Having caught a salmon in the famous fishery in Leenane, he brought it to Vincent in Westport to have it smoked. Vincent delivered it back out to the Delphi fishing lodge. He met Clapton out on the river casting his fly. 'And what did you say to him?' I asked Vincent excitedly. I was a bit disappointed when he told me. He had taken the opportunity to tell Eric Clapton, 'It's a funny old world'.

Andy Warhol was an artist who built a career on churning out stuff. He made a virtue of it, calling his studio the Factory, employing assistants (on little or no wages) to produce the work and celebrating the mass produced. I could not imagine him on Achillbeg. He liked the Isle of Manhattan.

I had been in Manhattan in 1969 but I never bumped into Andy Warhol. I remember seeing ads in the *Village Voice* proclaiming that 'Andy Warhol would endorse anything for money'. That sort of statement by an artist then was intended to be provocative and shocking. And, of course, ironic.

The year previously Warhol had been shot by one of his hangers-on and nearly died. This was the start of his later career where he was heavily managed and business-oriented. He embarked on his career as a celebrity and self-promoter. The art changed little from the early breakthrough style. When, years later, I was to see a substantial amount of Warhol work in London I was disappointed in it. The large scale of it and the slight effort used to produce it with the printing screens seemed excessive, even tacky. It reproduces well in books and magazines, though, which is probably appropriate for pop art. As a pop philosopher, if that is not a contradiction, he remains a guiding light.

I did some laundry to try out the clothes horse over the bath. It's an arrangement of drift wood and string on which I can hang clothes which will drip dry into the bath. Best thing I have ever made.

Some whittling on a knight. Bishops/rooks next. Storm warnings on the radio. The wind increases over the afternoon with the barometer falling. Hope I can get out for shopping tomorrow and, more importantly, that there is some money waiting at the post office. Out of powdered milk, all veggies, bread and all goodies like biscuits.

Chapter 7

A Hundred Milch Cows

Oro, sé do bheatha a bhaile,
is fearr liom tu ná céad bo bainne:
Oro, sé do bheatha a bhaile,
thá tu maith le rátha.

Oro, welcome home,
I would rather have you than a hundred milch cows:
Oro, welcome home,
'tis you are happy with prosperity
– Traditional

Friday, November 12

Blew a full gale last night and the punt was overturned down at the slip. I think that the punt must have been flipped by the wind as it was drying out on the shore. I had not thought that the wind was so strong from the noise and disturbance in the house. It's a solid, heavy boat, traditionally built by Pattons, a boatbuilding family in Saile, nearby. The same as would have been used by the islanders going back at least a hundred years.

I flipped it back right-side-up. I do this with the assistance of several props, gradually getting the gunnel off the ground and then my back under it and a final heave brings the hull sitting straight up on its side, the weight balanced. Then I sneak around to the keel side and let it roll back on to its bottom, upright. I take as much of the weight as I can off the keel and bilge as it falls.

The wind eased off somewhat by afternoon so went across for a shopping spree in Dereens. Luckily, there was some money in the post awaiting me. Bought lots of grub and had a nice drive around the locale in a car full of school kids with a local man who offered me a lift back to the pier as he delivered the kids to their homes on the school run.

Back at the house, letter reading. Looks like I may have to go to Dublin early (December 7th) if I am to take part in Christmas Art and Craft Fair.

Tooth giving me trouble. I tried to pull it out. No go. Now it is hanging out, secreting stuff and a bit painful. I just know I am going to get an abscess. In the old days, of course, when your teeth were gone, you died.

Saturday, November 13

Under the weather with toothache. Going to have to do something about it.

Sunday, November 14

Clean-up in the house then over to Corraun to mess about aboard *Molly B*, light the fire in the stove and relax for the afternoon. I find a phone in the pub and call Auntie Annette in Westport to try to get an appointment with a dentist. She tells me to come up to Westport.

Everything seems OK on board *Molly B*. Exciting trip back through choppy seas with the motor giving trouble. Strong wind from the west. At one stage I thought I might not make it back to Achillbeg but would have to land at Corraun and go back and spend the night on board *Molly B*. But with the help of the current, and dodging the worst of the breaking waves, I make the slip in one piece.

Monday, November 15

Trip to Westport. In afternoon rowed across to Cloghmore in the nine-foot tender. It's not too windy to use the light dinghy. It is easier to pull it out of the water and leave upside down at Cloghmore. I got a lift to Achill Sound where the manager of the Achill Sound Hotel arranged a lift to Newport for me. From there I hitched to Westport.

Tuesday, November 16

I browsed around Westport for the morning. I bought an Irish dictionary in the bookshop. I am trying to improve my hopeless Irish. (I still have that dictionary but my Irish speaking never took off.) Plus I bought Ann Chambers' biography of Granuaile which has just been published.

Appointment with dentist in the afternoon. He gets me out of my misery and puts me on antibiotics. He will have to do a complicated bridging job which will necessitate coming back a few times. Stayed on in Westport for the night.

Wednesday, November 17

The only member of my family who ever made it as an artist was Micheál de Búrca, 1913–1985, who was head of the National College of Art and Design (NCAD) from around 1942 to 1970. A long stint as Director by present-day practices. He was secretary of the RHA from 1948 to 1971.

He was an artist in the tradition of Keating and McGonigal under whom he had studied. He found himself head of the NCAD at a time of sweeping change and student revolt. This was the well documented strike and occupation of the art college in the late 1960s. The students went on strike, set up an alternative college, took off their clothes and chained themselves to the railings. Among their demands was that they called for Micheál de Búrca's head and got it from the fickle politicians. Micheál was not interested in reform, long hair and students running the art college. He retired to his native Mayo to end his days painting and relaxing. Uncle Vincent, who had known him well, had a lovely view of Killary Harbour in his living room which Micheál had painted. He appears to have worked much in Achill, and painted outdoors. This outdoor practice must have resulted in the sketchy and unfinished quality to much of his work.

I caught the 4.05 p.m. bus back to the wilds of Achill. I was picked up on the road to Cloghmore by a fisherman who had just come from Westport where he had been fishing oysters. I asked him had he any fish. He just had one scallop which was sitting proudly on the dash of his car like a manufacturer's mascot. I am sure he was looking forward to having it for dinner. King scallop is perhaps the finest seafood you can eat. Definitely. He presented it to me – a huge king scallop. 'You're a fish man are you?' he said. He dropped me off and told me to be careful with the crossing.

In the dark and in the small nine-foot tender, the crossing was feasible but initially scary. This was the little dinghy I had found abandoned in a skip in Vancouver. I had cut the hull to fit the shape of the deck of *Molly B* where it was stored upside down on top of the cabin. It had built-in buoyancy but not much freeboard, that is, sides, to keep the sea out. It could have filled with water quite easily. I feared conditions might get worse on the Achillbeg side where there is a rip, but in fact it improved as I got across into the shelter of the island.

I made it to the house by 7.00 p.m. and got the fire going. There was a funny smell in the house and I thought 'rats', but there seemed to be no sign. Perhaps it was half burnt garbage in the fire.

I had a gourmet meal. King scallop, caught that day, and rare roast beef sandwiches from McCormack's of Westport. 'Season of Plenty.'

Thursday, November 18

Good active day catching up after the depression of the toothache. Went down to the slip early to check on my boats and bring up my bag. All my pills from the dentist are ruined by rain water, as were two watercolour pads, one with some paintings in it. Well not ruined, changed. Windy, showery day and a bad forecast. Storm.

Friday, November 19

Blew stink overnight, rattling the roof and the rain pelting the Plexiglas window of my bedroom. Keeping me awake. Arose late (10.00) and had a good day at the artwork. Windy and sunny all day, the wind decreasing in the evening. Did not even think of going out to Dereens. Will wait until next week.

Saturday, November 20

Mild, windy day. Mild enough to do some stone moving down at the slip, clearing the beach where the punt rests to make a clean berth for it. The strong current keeps replacing the stones I clear.

Back at the house whittling on the chess set. I finish one side and therefore the design of the chess set.

This is the third chess set I have made. The first one was commissioned by the mother of Nigel, a friend in college, when she heard that I did such things. She was a good, earnest woman from Belfast and wanted to encourage me. The pieces were based on Irish medieval carvings scattered all over the country. I copied them from art books, magazines and postcards. She lived in England and I used to send the pieces to her three or four at a time so I never saw the full set as a unit.

The second set was based on modernist design like that of the Bauhaus. It was much easier and faster to make. I gave it to a girlfriend. This third chess set (which I am working on) I ended up mounting on a chess board, screwing the pieces in place and framing it so that it became a piece of relief sculpture. You couldn't play a game of chess with it. I sold it through the Kenny Gallery in Galway as I did with most of the carving I did on the island that winter. I am sorry now that I do not have a photo of that third chess set.

Sunday, November 21

I was awakened in the still of the calm night by the sound of the wind suddenly coming on at a gale force blast. It was still blowing gale force in the morning so did not cross over for Mass. It would have been possible to make the crossing but I felt prudence in the face of the locals was a better decision. They would probably like to worship in peace anyway.

Peadar O'Donnell (1893–1986) had come to Achill to convert the people to Communism. He worked among the tatie hokers in Scotland, many of whom came from Achill and his native Donegal. He did not have a lot of luck in Achill where the church spoke out against him. Somewhat surprisingly, Peadar O'Donnell was my godfather, though I did not know it for many years. I don't think he ever much knew himself that he had the honour of being my godfather.

Following a long career of agitation, membership of the IRA and imprisonment he had become editor of the *Bell* magazine in Dublin in his later career as a writer. My mother, as a young girl up in Dublin from Westport, had somehow landed the job as secretary/receptionist to the literary magazine. She even met her husband through the connection. My father had worked as an engineer for an electrical company which took out advertising in the *Bell*. It must have been on his visits to the magazine to pay a bill or to deliver copy that he got to know the receptionist! Perhaps when I came along it might have seemed like a good career initiative to ask the venerable editor to be my godfather!

Around this time I approached Peadar O'Donnell and reminded him of the fact that I was his godson. He invited me to a meeting of the Irish Communist Party. To which I did not go.

Peadar ODonnell's books on the rural Irish I find difficult to read. They are a bit didactic and de Valeran in their promotion of the pure rural ideal. The comely maidens and dancing at the crossroads sort of stuff.

Monday, November 22

It blew stink and rained all night and morning. The back room where I am sleeping is a mess. The wall is saturated with water. While the plastic sheet in front of the window keeps out the wind-blown rain, the wall is full to overflowing with water. It seeps down and pools on the floor. Perhaps some tar on the outside would help to seal it. The roof too is leaking with the slates blowing off. My makeshift repairs, concentrated in this area, cannot withstand the wind.

I am painting business cards. Lots of them. Business cards might be the new next big thing.

Wind eases in the evening so perhaps we will have a run to Achill Sound on the morrow. Need lots of glass.

Tuesday, November 23

Nice still night and then confused mess of a day, mainly caused by getting up late and thinking I was early. Clock was two hours wrong.

Attempted a run to Achill Sound in the punt but the motor was giving trouble so I turned back from just past Granuaile's castle. Brought motor up to the house and gave it a bit of a service. A cold day and feeling a bit lethargic. Some painting and whittling.

A mouse or small rat in the kitchen this evening. It did not notice that I was dozing on the sofa. It did a tour of the living room, checking out my boots in front of the fire before disappearing under the fridge. What to do? I don't know where it could be getting in and I don't want a big bloodthirsty battle ...

Wednesday, November 24

Up latish (10.00) but a productive morning's work. Mainly framing. Headache in the afternoon slowed things down. I got the derelict house next door sealed from rain by covering the windows with scrap linoleum. Now I wonder if I could rent or buy it. It is identical to the one I am living in and would make an excellent studio. One would have it completely empty and just have an electricity supply and water. Excellent for work. Almost worth driving a taxi in Toronto to get the money to pay for it. I'm already restricted in the present house. Things piling up everywhere. Oh, to be a Big Name Artist! Apprentices, equipment, proposals, agents, managers. Celebrity, retrospectives, books, invitations, interviews. 'Fame, I'm going to live forever' was then a popular song spawned by the hit movie.

I put another item in a bottle. A small whittling of a girl's head in a horseradish bottle, then mounted to become a candle holder. At least I have finished this one and can use it when the electricity fails.

Did some paintings of broken bottles. I had recently seen a big exhibition of Morandi etchings and thought broken bottles might be an original take on his signature subject matter. Though I don't

think broken bottles as a subject are going to last. I am clearing up hundreds of bottles from the dump area and breaking them into the rubble beneath the patio. I have this theory that it will discourage rats and mice from burrowing under there. Of course, it also gets rid of the decade's long build-up of beer, wine, milk and liqueur bottles stored in the dump. Years of serious drinking. It is said that there are no rats on one of the Inishkea islands because the sand there is sharp and that the rats do not like that.

Thursday, November 25

Sunny day but also some rain and wind getting up in the evening. Heinrich Böll is associated with Achill but there is no record of him ever visiting Achillbeg. He visited Achill from about 1950 and was awarded the Nobel Prize in 1972. He left his house in Dugort as an artist's retreat. He was appreciative of the local people and their response to the madness of the world, which had produced the wars in which Böll had been forced to fight. He was fond of the Irish saying, 'When God made time, he made plenty of it'.

Friday, November 26

Did a trial run with my electric drying rack. It's a lethal construction consisting of an ancient electric bar heater which is covered by a plastic tent strung between two chairs. Into this are inserted oil paintings and wet, varnished frames. A strong stench of varnish solvent, presumably highly imflammable, pervades the room. If it does not burn the house down or knock me out from fumes, it should work. I had been having difficulty getting varnish to dry.

Beautiful, calm, cold day with filtered sun so I set off with the flooding tide up to Achill Sound.

Sweeney's hardware shop took ages to deliver some glass. They have to cut it for me. They like to keep me hanging around there to observe me, I suspect. 'When God made time, he made plenty of it.' If it's good enough for Böll, it's good enough for me.

Sweeney's gave me a good deal on the sale of some scrap plywood doors which I can use for framing. They had a huge collection of them in a back room, many of them a bit damaged. It cost £2.00 for a door which would have had at least £8.00 worth of plywood in it. I will have to break them up but there is also other wood in the doors which will be usable.

I had a nice chat with my relative Michael Lavelle in his shop in the Sound. He brought me home to his house for a super midday meal of potatoes and lamb and white cheese sauce. He has a good library back in his house and he lends me some books.

Over at the fish co-op, which is in one of the old train station buildings, I found a nice piece of halibut. The young lad there gives me a great discount. The fish is £1.25 a pound. Its weight comes to more than four pounds and he says, 'Give me £4.00'. I ask him if he has any oysters. They are £2.00 a kilo. He gives me about a dozen oysters and charges me £1. He is smoking a cigarette in a very showy way, all the proper hand holds, inhales, pauses and gestures of the seasoned gangster smoker. I tell him he should give up smoking. He says he has tried to give it up 'many times'. He is about 14 years old!

It is a beautiful trip back down the sound with the ebb tide, into the dusk and sunset. The punt is full of plywood doors, glass, food, books and fish. I feel good. Master of my universe. There is snow on the mountains to the northeast. A definite snow line half way up their summit. Beautiful crisp colours from sea to sky. That might be Nephin Beg to the north. Corraun Hill abeam and the tip of Croagh Patrick, as always, keeping watch over the bay.

I stop at the pub at Dereens. A man there asks me why I do not collect the dole. 'Everyone else does,' he says, in a friendly way. Great Artists Living on Islands do not collect the dole.

There is a message from the dentist giving me an appointment on Monday. Also confirmation from the Dublin Art and Craft fair at

Christmas. My sister is responsible for suggesting my involvement with this cooperative effort by a bunch of Irish craftspeople and artists. It will be a four-day exhibition in the Mansion House, Dublin, aimed at the Christmas gift market. I had been thinking more of an invitation from the Museum of Modern Art in New York or the Tate in London, but for now the Dublin Mansion House Christmas Craft Fair would have to do. A Great Artist should be able to show . . . well . . . anywhere!

Saturday, November 27

A busy day. Down to the slip early (8.30) to collect a load of things bought yesterday. Then a big framing effort most of the day.

The teak frames I made that winter I thought were lovely. The best things I ever made. Most were 'box' frames where there is a space between the glass and the artwork. Sometimes I accentuated this space by using screws or nails or other fastenings to hold the artwork in position. A bit like notes pinned to a notice board. At other times I further accentuated the space by leaving something in the frame such as an old tooth brush or a disposable lighter screwed defiantly on top of the artwork. I'm not sure why I chose toothbrushes (and ones which had obviously been used at that) but it was partly humorous. The plastic handles of the toothbrushes were colourful. I thought that the technology of the disposable lighter was so beautiful and perfect that I could not throw them away. Again, they were colourful on top of the monochrome drawings. Maybe it was a comment on recycling, then gaining traction as a lifestyle choice. Maybe it was a reference to the joke, or cliché, about the surgeon leaving an implement inside a patient.

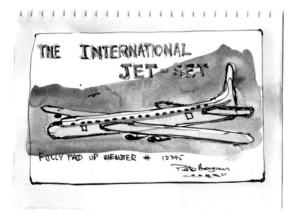

I liked them, but again, they were not a great commercial success. I could not understand why somebody might not think a used toothbrush screwed to a picture inside a frame was not something unique and desirable. In fact, they were difficult to give away. I said to myself, 'I should charge ridiculously high prices for these. Then people will take them seriously.'

Drawing and painting all evening. Business cards – Rent a

Crowd Ltd. Rent an Irish Cottage, Achillbeg Laundry Company, Goldfingers, and so on) Bed after midnight, tired.

The idea of painting business cards was also an inspired one I thought. Combining Warhollian irony with Irish wit. Having studied Business Studies in Trinity College, Dublin, I felt qualified. The cards had to have a strong graphic input, that is, a picture of some sort. The business title usually involved some sort of double entendre. There was always a humorous reading. They took very little time to paint but then were framed which took a lot longer. They

were also about identity. I think I was influenced by the well-known English pop artist Joe Tilson whose work I had seen in Vancouver.

Sunday, November 28

I went over to Corraun harbour in the afternoon to check on *Molly B*. I ran into John Winnie, the skipper of the *Inish Arcain* who I had met the first night I went over there. He showed me the engine of *Inish Arcain* which he keeps in top condition. It's a 1957 Kelvin diesel and he has it ticking away like a sewing machine. His boat would be ideal for an Irish fishing boat conversion to a yacht/motor sailer. It is the right size, 50 foot, and has the style, having being built in Arklow by the famous Tyrell yard.

He came aboard *Molly B* and talked at great length and in good cheer. He is not intimidated by the small, cramped cabin, being well accustomed to boats and the ways of the sea. He says he would encourage his three sons, presently in school, to leave Corraun. He had a good suggestion about lobster fishing from the shore which I wanted to try. He said to throw in the pot opposite the 'White Elephant' which he calls the beacon at the entrance. I have some bait now so must try it. The Achillbeg people, in the old days when there was no roads on the island, used always to walk in Indian file or, as he said, 'like ducks'. They were all tall, he said. 'Half of Cleveland is owned by Corraun people,' he said proudly.

Monday, November 29

Dental appointment in Westport. I tripped the punt out yesterday at the slip so it would be afloat in the morning. Over to Cloghmore and got a lift almost immediately from a man, I forget his name, who keeps sheep in Achillbeg and who doesn't get on very well with me. He calls me 'sir'. I got to the sound early so tried doing a sketch of the bridge while waiting for the bus. Achill Sound village is a difficult place to sketch or paint. Nothing very prominent, it is very flat, and there is no focus of attention. The bridge should be the obvious interest but it is not very remarkable in appearance. People, typically tourists, driving across the bridge often miss it and do not realise they are on an island.

The dentist in Westport packs my mouth full of solid gold for three hours and I miss the bus back to Achill. I meet Aunt Annette, Aunt Clare, Katrina, Mary Clare, Michael, John, Ann Magella, Sarah, Aunt Brigit, Aunt Anne, and Uncle Vincent. They stuff me full of wonderful food.

Tuesday, November 30

Spent the day sketching around Westport. I sneaked into the grounds of Westport House to do a picture of the front facade. I got a haircut and then caught the 4.05 p.m. bus back to Achill Sound. I walked half way to Cloghmore when an inquisitive man picked me up and went out of his way to drop me to the pier at Cloghmore. He said he has seen me around and that he had done work on the electricity on the houses in Achillbeg. 'You must be a hard man to stay in there,' he said.

Was back at the house by 7.00 p.m. and had a big tuck-in to Auntie Annette's porter cake.

Chapter 8

A Visitor

I've just called in to see you all,
I'll only stay a while.
I want to see how you're getting on,
I want to see you smile.
– Seán McBride

Wednesday, December 1

Up late (9.30) but made up for it with productive day. A big batch (16) of one design frames varnished and on to the drying racks, hopefully for last coat of varnish. The drying rack is in the back bedroom in which I sleep. I hope I don't get high on varnish fumes tonight or have nightmares or something.

Did some laundry and set a lobster pot at the slip at low tide using pieces of rotten turbot as bait. I look forward to a piece of lobster tomorrow at midday. Three local half-deckers arrive back from Westport. The oyster season must have finished. They made a fine sight entering on the bottom of the tide as they gunned their engines upstream across the bar. Did some repair to Vincent's motor which broke the other day. And a lot of painting. Bed at 12.30.

Thursday, December 2

Nice calm but grey day. Not too cold. I was painting away in the house when Georganna walks in the door. What a surprise! She got a lift across to the island with Martin Kilbane who she met at the pier. It's impressive that she found her way this far. We discuss old times and new times and go for a walk around the island to show it to her.

Georganna had come to Europe in the entourage of the Dali Lama. He likes to travel in the company of advisors, sympathetic souls and artists. Thus, Georganna had been invited to tag along. Part of the deal was a Eurorail pass on trains all over Europe for the entourage. Georganna had realised that this pass was valid for Ireland. On

some time off from being with the entourage of the Dali Lama she had decided to visit what she felt sure would be a bustling art commune on an island on the west coast of Ireland. I might be a bit responsible for this vision of Achillbeg on Georganna's part, having corresponded with her. But I am sure I did not mislead her! She assumed that the west of Ireland might be a bit like the Pacific Northwest, only a bit more 'olde worlde'. I think she was a bit disappointed by the bleakness of it all when she finally saw it. She was accustomed to trees and sea eagles, bears, Indians and totem poles, pickup trucks and log cabins. Music, argument and lots of action. Here she found stone walls, stoicism, cold and emptiness.

I had met Georganna Malloff in Vancouver. She was part of the wave of hippies and alternative types who moved north to Canada from the US to avoid the draft for the Vietnam war. In Vancouver she was carving a totem pole. It was not an Indian-style totem pole from the Pacific Northwest but what she described as a Cosmic Maypole. Her work was more in the tradition of western art rather than the natives

of the region. In Vancouver, when I had met her, she was in control of a huge aircraft hangar in which several artists had studios. They were happy to give me a studio and I started making art. Very happily, for about three years.

A classic dispute developed between the owner of the hangar, Vancouver City, and the squatting artists. The artists were evicted. Georganna's pole was erected in the city of New Westminster in British Columbia and is still there. She retreated to an island in the Gulf of Georgia. I built the *Molly B* and sailed off to Ireland.

Georganna had met and studied art under Dudley Carter, a famous Pacific Northwest carver. He in turn had worked under the influence of the great Diego Rivera when Rivera visited San Francisco in 1940 and worked there. So Georganna had a great pedigree in public art and there are similarities in the work of all three artists.

Friday, December 3

I sat around talking to, and being inspired by, Georganna all day. She is hoping to motivate me to do some sort of art project here under her guidance, similar to a project she did in Toronto with some carvers. I'm not really her apprentice but she might not accept that!

I make a run out to the post office for letters and supplies. I check the lobster pot thinking it would be nice to present Georganna with a lobster dinner. It turns out to be a disappointment, full of small crabs. No edible crab and certainly no lobster.

Over at Cloghmore pier the co-op manager was busy dumping boxes of whiting into the water. They had been bought by the EEC who did not wish to try to market them. The EEC buys them to subsidise the fishermen, and then they are thrown overboard into the sea. I got a couple of whiting and a squid for free.

Saturday, December 4

More talking with Georganna who doesn't stir far from the fire or her bed. The cold and the food are starting to get to her. The only thing she likes in the larder is jam eaten straight from the jar with a spoon. She consults her large armoury of maps and bus and ferry timetables and decides she has to try to get to Rosslare Port in County Wexford by Sunday. 'There's nothing much happening around here,' she declares. I explain to her the difficult logistics of public transport in this part of the universe. To try to get to Rosslare by the following day on public transport I deem to be impossible. She will not be dissuaded ...

Around 3.00 p.m. we head up the sound in the punt to help her find a lift to Westport. From Dereens I call ahead to Vincent in Westport who invites her to stay for the night. Georganna has calculated that if she can catch the morning train out of Westport she can make her connection.

It's about two hours after low water with the flooding tide and we have difficulty getting to Achill Sound in the punt. We run into shallows below Achill Sound and I spend about half an hour up to my thighs in the water pulling us forward on the sandbanks with the

keel sticking in sand. Georganna sits regally in the stern urging me on. We abandon the punt near Achill Sound and land on the shore. We walk across the fields and up to the pubs at the sound. It is getting dark. Georganna is shocked to see the interior of an Achill pub in the off-season. She had expected jolly fellows in soft hats playing fiddles. *Ceol agus craic agus rula bula.* We were met by silent, sullen male stares in the smoky interiors.

We ask around for a lift towards Westport. No go. In the pub someone gives me a newspaper cutting about myself from *The Irish Times.* It's part of the publicity from the Art and Craft Fair. Georganna shows around pictures of her work. She has a handy portfolio which she whips out at the least provocation.

We try hitching on the main road out of the island but again no luck. Then we return to the pub for hot whiskies and decide to head back to Achillbeg, me complaining about my cold, wet legs. Perhaps because of the hot whiskies, Georganna decides to come along back to the island though she is very anxious to get to her ferry. The next ferry which will make all her connections is three days away, and she is not looking forward to three more days on Achillbeg Island.

We find the punt where we left it and set off back down the sound in the dark. The tide by now is falling. It's dark. We hit a sand bank, the motor ploughs into the sand. The shear pin on the propeller breaks so we now have no motor power. I start rowing and we make good time with the help of the ebbing tide.

About a mile later as we draw abreast of Dereens, the distant twinkling lights of Pattens, the pub, start to appeal to Georganna. The effect of the whiskies dies off, plus she starts to think of another two days on freezing, windy Achillbeg. She decides, for better or worse, she must go ashore. 'I'll walk to Westport,' she says. I try to dissuade her but she is 'not going back to that island'. She insists on going ashore and taking her chances. We land opposite the church at Dereens and walk back to Pattens pub where we meet a couple getting into their car and going as far as Achill Sound. They agree to take her. I say good bye to her and, never expecting to see Georganna again, she heads off into the night.

I walked back through the fields to the punt. I set off and rowed the mile or so to the slip on Achillbeg, a nice row in the calm night, luckily with the tidal current helping me along. I arrived at the house at about 11.00 p.m. Warmed up by my exertions I got out of my wet clothes and breathed a sigh of relief.

I don't like the sort of upset with the locals which something like the above causes.

I hope Georganna is OK. I told her to find a bed and breakfast for the night. It's certainly safe to be wandering around at night in Achill as a woman on her own. There is not much danger, but it could cause a bit of a stir. Hippies doing odd things in the middle of the night and all that. Being conspicuous!

Sunday, December 5

Up to catch the late Mass at Dereens. There I expected someone to accost me any minute with tales of disaster and Georganna the previous night. But there was nothing. I wonder how she has fared on her journey. Someone told me about my name being mentioned on *The Late Late Show* on telly last night as part of the publicity effort for the Craft Fair. 'The Artist on the Island.' Well, that's got to be good.

Back at the house the excitement of exhibiting was taking over. Have to forget about Georganna for a while. I spent all day framing and packing and even painting and was nearly finished by 1.30 a.m. the following morning.

Monday, December 6

I am astir early, packing and lugging 'stuff' down to the slip. It's a beautiful, frosty, clear, calm morning. 'I'm off to Dublin'.

I had quite a job getting everything down to the slip. There were three big packages of artwork and a couple of bags. I left a rucksack and a pair of shoes under the currach wreck.

I rowed across in the punt with my packages and got a lift up to Achill Sound. I then caught the early bus to Westport.

I had time to call to Uncle Vincent and got news of Georganna's trip away from Achillbeg. When I left her she had a lift to Achill Sound from the pub. Somehow at Achill Sound she got a lift to Newport in a Garda car! Vincent was hazy on the details. The Garda picked her up as she was hitching and dropped her in Newport some twenty miles down the road, he thought. I am sure the Garda must have been interested in what she was up to. Then she hitched, or perhaps got a taxi, from there to Westport. There are not many taxis in this part of the world. She stayed the night with Vincent whom I had told her to look up. From there she headed off on the train to catch her ferry at Rosslare to take her back to the Dali Lama. The Dali Lama and his entourage were visiting the Pope!

Some months later I approached the Galway Arts Officer with a proposal that Galway should fund one of Georganna's carving projects. The Galway Arts Officer was horrified. 'We don't want any totem poles around here,' she said.

Georganna Maloff is still in the Pacific Northwest, still working away on her carving and her art.

From Westport I got the train to Dublin and the Art and Craft Fair. It's a welcome break from being the Artist on the Island. I sell some of my works and make some much needed money. I am a minor celebrity, very minor.

Life is easier in the city. Its two weeks to go until Christmas. I don't have the energy or the courage to force myself back to Achill. Back to the wind and the rain and the damp, the limpets and the turf, the sheep and the fox, the struggle and the strangeness.

Life in the city is good, if a bit artificial. I am in my snooker craze phase. It is the era of Alex 'Hurricane' Higgins, my hero. My friend Aidan and I find a sleazy snooker hall off Dame Street and while away the hours potting balls, then retire to the Stags Head pub next door for pints and talk. Across Dame Street in the Temple Bar area they are planning to build a huge bus station. Aidan is looking for a studio among all the rundown buildings slated for demolition.

I had met Aidan in the life drawing workshop of the art club of Trinity College. Brian Bourke used to tutor the class. He would not let the model stay stationary, insisting that he or she move slowly while we tried to draw. 'Draw fast, fast!' he would say. 'Ya got to draw fast. Speed produces style.' And that was my art education, in a nutshell.

Chapter 9

Riders to the Sea

'They are all gone now, and there isn't
anything more the sea can do to me.'
– J.M. Synge

Tuesday, January 4, 1983

I arrived back to Westport from Dublin on the train to find that the dentist will 'do' me on the morrow. The dentist, John Campbell, is very understanding and asks me to give him a piece of art in exchange for dentistry.

Storm force winds keep me in Westport following my visit to John. Then, on Thursday, I caught the afternoon bus to Achill. It's still blowing hard, raining, and it's dark, of course. I judge the conditions too extreme to launch the punt and row across to Achillbeg. Instead I get off the bus at the turn-off for Corraun. I walk the three miles to the harbour there and stay the night on board *Molly B*.

It was a pleasant, comfortable night in the tiny harbour. Once the stove is lit, the interior heats up and I feel at home. Rain patters on the deck, the wind howls in the rigging of the fishing boats alongside. The headlights of cars, the glimmer from cottages and the harbour lights glisten in the dark. More people should live on boats. The tide lifts the hull and gently rocks me to sleep. A few hours later the tide gently deposits *Molly B* back on to the mud. A newcomer to the harbour, a 35-foot half-decker is bumping the bow of *Molly B*. I adjust the lines. It's like the good old days – living on board.

I walked and hitched into Achill Sound the following morning. I called into the Garda station and thanked the guard on duty for helping Georganna to get off the island, as I assume they did. 'Right so,' he says and not much else. I wasn't quite sure if he knew what I was talking about. I then got picked up by Pádraig and brought to Cloghmore via Pattens. Tea in Kilbanes.

Had a stiff row across to the slip into fresh, windy conditions. That was the right decision the previous night – to stay on the mainland.

Minor disaster at the slip. The wind has blown away the rucksack which had a pair of shoes in it from where it was stashed in the turf store. The rucksack was the main method for bringing up the turf to the house and so is a bit of a loss. Also the shoes. The wind at the slip does funny things.

I arrived at the house finally at 2.00 p.m. Four days, door to door! There was no evidence of rats in the house, which is a relief. They tend to make their way indoors for the winter. The house seems very damp and cold. I light the fire. A cup of tea and then a search along the shore in vain for the missing rucksack.

Saturday, January 8

Up latish to windy, cold, dull day. January is a windy month. Much letter writing following a big batch of post picked up at the post office yesterday. Mainly from my fans overseas, Christmas greetings, and so on.

Nothing much of interest has blown up on the rocky beach following the long Christmas break. At the slip I fixed up the currach turf shelter which had been blown away, cleared more stones from the beach there and retied down the small tender. I think I am lucky that it was not blown away. Now using a poly sack to get turf up to the house. That is how I am going to have to do it until I get another rucksack. It doesn't work too bad and is less weight when it is empty. I fixed the prop on the outboard which had been broken on the Georganna escapade.

Wind builds up over the day to Force 8 and the barometer is falling. Cold, even sitting close to the fire. I might build a door from the porch into the main room to give a bit more insulation.

Sunday, January 9

Latish awake. Wind still fresh though eased off from last night. Big clean-up in the house.

I walked around to the slip by the west side of the island. That's the long way around. A distance of about two miles depending on the route one takes. Past Mrs. Boydell's house, past the Holy Well and past the promontory fort. There is a wonderful dramatic view out to the west across the storm-tossed sea. Out in the middle, defying the waves, is the Bills Rock. Michael Viney spent a weekend out there counting the petrels. Fair dues to him. The British Navy, pre-World War I, used it for target practice. They apparently bought it from the Pike estate, a big local landowner, for use as target practice. Now Bills Rock is home to a large number of storm petrels. Below the surface out there is reputed to be a huge colony of crayfish.

If James Joyce was an island he would have to be Bills Rock. Alone it stands out there in the full, deep Atlantic, immovable and impregnable, dark, isolated and unattainable.

To the north along the Achill shore is the Atlantic Drive, and at the end of it the twin triangles of Keem Bay and the cliffs behind. Higher and more dramatic than those at Moher. A magnificent vista.

The deep coves on the west side of Achillbeg are completely full of foam stirred up by the confused sea. Like a badly poured pint of porter. One could have waded into the foam way over one's head if the wind was not so strong. The top of the foam blows off downwind leaving streaks of white on the dark green grass of the fields. Spindrift.

Some of the most interesting abandoned cottages are on the north side of Achillbeg. There they stand opposite the Blind Sound like mini-pyramids, monuments to a previous era. All the plaster and mortar and roof beams are gone. Most would have been thatched. The fireplaces, with impressive dry stonework, dominate the small interior rooms. The wind whistles through the walls. The people are in Cleveland. Who can blame them?

The punt at the slip had flipped again and was floating upside down. Perhaps because it was tied too tightly by me yesterday. I assume that it gets caught in a circular squall coming down from the hill, and then flips in the steep waves. The waves build up because there is a strong current running out against the westerly wind on the ebb. The punt is quite heavy and also would have some water in it, making it heavier. So it must be quite a dramatic scene when it flips in the wind.

The punt is in a sorry state. It got badly scraped on its aft starboard transom edge as it sat on the slip at Cloghmore over Christmas. I have to repair that and it could do with a coat of paint. Also it has lost a bilge rubbing strip and one of the ribs amidships seems loose.

Monday, January 10

Windy, grey day. Southwest gales forecast on the radio but it's mild. Also on the radio in the evening I catch a short item: 'Three farmers in Achill believed washed out to sea.' That short item dominates the day and I remain glued to the news bulletins on the radio for the following days. But there is no further information. Where could that have happened? I hope it is not on the Cloghmore side of the island. There are many cliffs on the Atlantic Drive nearby. The news affects me strangely, like losing someone close, even though I have no further information.

I'm running low on turf at the house. My stockpile, stored in the house next door, has been much depleted during the visit of Georganna. The lack of a rucksack to haul it up from the slip means it is

more of a chore to move it. Bringing it up by polysack is almost as much work as the old wheelbarrow. The ground is too soft to use the wheelbarrow again. The wheel sinks into the mud up to its axel. I am burning up turf faster than I can bring it up from the slip.

I did a good five hours and more of carving. Working on a sheep carving, a group of shawlie woman, a torso and an odd sort of bird. The carving keeps me warm.

No chance of getting over to Corraun to check on *Molly B*. The wind blows relentlessly, the waves break across the bar, the sheep huddle in the lee of the stone walls. Everywhere is grey. There is no horizon line out to the west. Where the sky meets the sea is just a fuzzy transition. The hillsides are a dark red colour, turf, even sepia. There is no growth. The rain runs down the hillside in white tor-

rents and ponds up into lakes on the sodden ground in the valley. There is a big river running down to the sea at the beach from the central valley. It's like a textbook model of how erosion happens.

Inside the house the cold seeps through into my back through my layers of jumpers, shirts and vest as I sit hunched over the smoldering fire. It's a big effort to go outside. The slates rattle on the roof. The rain spatters against the windows and the window frames clatter. The draughts permeate everywhere. It feels like it could blow like this for a month. Forever.

And somewhere out there, three local men, tending their sheep, have been blown off the rocks to their deaths. Cast a cold eye. Making art, painting pictures or whittling silly pieces of driftwood seems like a totally irrelevant, even irreverent, thing to be doing.

Tuesday, January 11

Another wild, windy night. I'm wrapped up in a sleeping bag and three blankets carefully arranged over and tucked in so as not to leak in the cold. I toss and turn in a semi-trance, listening to the noise. I feel like a mountaineer on K2 or Apsley Cherry-Garrard out on the Beardmore Glacier. As the dawn breaks there is no inducement to get up at all except for the drips of rain coming in from the ceiling, splashing on to the bed and making a pool on the floor, wetting the blankets.

I am sleeping on the lower level of a bunk bed, a steel contraption suitable for kids in a holiday home. On the top bunk lie the masts of *Molly B* which have come in the window and stretch the length of the bedroom, extend through the open doorway and are propped up by the book shelf at the far end of the living room. It might be a cosy situation if there were no draughts and no leaks from the roof. But it's at the west end of the house which takes the full battering of the wind and rain. Here also the roof is most permeable and has lost most slates. I think I will have to abandon the back room as a place to sleep and move into the living room. The dark morning light comes late.

I went down to the slip at midday. More drama. The punt was overturned again by the wind. It must have landed on a stone as a hole had been punched in its side. This despite my efforts clearing stones away from where the punt lies at low tide. With much effort I moved it up to the high water mark and left it upside-down. I thought I heard car horns beeping from over the other side at Cloghmore, but I could see no sign of any action there. Maybe I'm going mad.

On the national news at 1.30 p.m., there is a report that three Achill sheep farmers have been lost from cliffs at the foot of Slievemore. That's the north side of Achill Island. They were attempting to rescue sheep from the cliffs. This is serious.

Carving and frame making and down for a second load of turf in late afternoon as the wind dies down. The wind increases again by

night and is presently blowing Force 7 and it's raining. It's been very dark today also, even at noon it felt like the sun had forgotten, or not bothered, to get out of bed.

Thinking about it, I am reassured that January will probably be the worst month for weather on the island. This is liable to be as bad as it can get. I have got to stick with it. Anyway, there is nowhere I can go.

I am not the first 'blow in' to stay a winter on Achillbeg. Some years before me an English couple, called Chris and Ann, spent a winter in their cottage on the far side of the beach. I can see the cottage out of my living room window. I take my hat off to them as they did it with no electricity supply. At least they had each other to keep themselves warm! They came to Achill on their honeymoon, found the house on Achillbeg and stayed for the winter. Their house has a wonderful situation on the island, overlooking the beach like the Paorach's which is nearby.

Wednesday, January 12

I moved into the main living room to sleep on the sofa in front of the smoldering fire last night. It was a cold night. Wind abated and rain stopped in the morning. I discovered about four slates missing from the roof, including one where a bad leak in the back room has developed.

Down at the slip I did a reasonable plywood-and-tar repair to the punt where it was holed. This will allow me to use it. I slapped on a bit of paint and also did a repair to the rubbing strip on the tender.

Back at the house I had an unexpected visit at about 4.00 p.m. from Joe the German and an artsy friend of his. They brought along with them an Austrian artist called Turi Werkner. Turi had, for some reason, turned up in Achill. Maybe he had read Heinrich Böll. Achill is popular with Germans. Because Turi spoke German they had introduced him to Joe the German. Joe thought Turi would like to meet the Artist on the Island. So they took a currach over from Granuaile's castle and visited me as a sort of outing.

They did not stay long as they had been delayed getting here. Plus it was getting dark. Turi seemed like a witty, cosmopolitan sort and apparently is a successful artist in Europe, mainly Germany and Austria. He had a nice smile as he rolled his own cigarettes using black paper. I walked down to the slip with them, glad of the company and the chat. They have news of the three men washed off the foot of Slievemore. Still no bodies have been recovered.

Thursday, January 13

Up latish on cold sunny morning and got out and did some road drainage work on the section sloping down to the sea. When it rains heavily that section of the road is like a stream. Espied a couple of fishing boats going out. It's still a bit windy though. I flipped the overturned punt which I had repaired and launched it. I brought down the motor in preparation for tomorrow. Back in the house I did some carving but it's a slowish, depressing day. It's cold, it's windy, it's wet. There's no end in sight and three people are dead.

Friday, January 14

Down early to the punt to try to catch the tide, the timing of which is unsuitable these days. Its high water at 6.00 a.m., meaning it's out all day. The boat was high and dry so I left it till 2.00 p.m. and came back and moved the punt, end by end, crab fashion, down the beach to the water. It's the only way I can move it and quite an effort. I crossed over to Cloghmore in the stiff wind to do some shopping.

Got a lift half way to Dereens by the school bus driver who often gives me lifts. I gave him £1.00 as people often pay him for lifts in an informal sort of way. Not much post. One important letter from dentist John Campbell who confirms that he would like a piece of art in exchange for his dental work. This is a big help.

I ended up giving John Campbell the figurehead of *Molly B*. This was a carved head in what I thought was the Egyptian style. It was a carving which I had done in Vancouver of a sort of androgynous face with big hair. It just happened to fit perfectly under the bowsprit on *Molly B*. With a bit of imagination it might perhaps have been a representation of a young Molly Bloom. I took it off the hull, mounted it on a plaque and gave it to John.

I had a pint in Pattens and then a lift back to Cloghmore with the crew of the *Honey Bee* fishing boat.

Saturday, January 15

I planned a trip over to *Molly B* in Corraun harbour but the punt was high and dry again with the tides so abandoned the venture thinking that next week would be better anyway.

Dull, mild day. Did some carving and replaced the worst slate missing on the roof with the single spare slate that I have.

Finished reading autobiography of George A. Birmingham, a.k.a. the Rev. Hannay, parson of Westport for 21 years from around 1900. Un-put-down-able. He was a strong character, not afraid of a fight with the local, majority religion. He wrote several books set in the Clew Bay region.

Sunday, January 16

I went out in the punt to Dereens. I was hoping to get some news of the search for the sheep farmers but there was none. The search for the bodies is still ongoing.

Stiff row back against the wind as motor ran out of petrol on the way over. The petrol must have leaked out of the tank while the motor was stored. Windy, misty, sunny day with a gale warning on the radio.

I did a big clean-up back in the house and some rearrangements as I move a few more bits of redundant furniture to the house next door. The main room was getting a bit cluttered. Plan to return to sleep in the back room now that the hole in the roof is at least partially fixed. I have the heater drying it out and drying frames in there at the moment.

I found one of the shoes which I lost at the slip. But only one, which is not much use. A delicious meal of a roast chicken in the evening. I should have invited my girlfriend around to share it!

Chapter 10

Imagine

Imagine there's no heaven
It's easy if you try
No hell below us
Above us only sky.
– John Lennon

Monday, January 17

Windy and a bit of rain. The best day's work yet. I started by liberating the porch, throwing out a long curved bench which dominated it. The porch tends to become cluttered and full of coats, boots, firewood and shovels. Spent the day building a super carving easel and turning the porch into a handy mini-carving studio. The easel is not as fancy as the one I left in Vancouver, but given the materials it's OK. It dominates the centre of the space and allows me to carve in the round, and to see the work in a beautiful setting.

I considered the possibility of putting a plastic curtain right across the middle of the living room to make one half of it easier to heat. That is what Eskimos do. They build their tents, made of animal skins, inside igloos, giving them a version of double glazing. But maybe the worst of the cold part of the year is over.

Over at Cloghmore pier the *Honey Bee* was beached as they worked on the hull. The *Honey Bee* is a fine big, old, traditional Scottish-built trawler.

Tuesday, January 18

Cold windy day with hail. Carving on the new easel. The easel is very successful as it allows me to keep a carving permanently in situ and visible and workable as I go about my day. I can walk around it, 360 degrees. The light is also very good with the two big windows of the porch. It's almost like being outside.

I have a pleasant run over to Corraun to pick up luggage stashed on *Molly B*. Did some shopping in the pub. I told the man who lives at the harbour that I would sell *Molly B* for £10,000. And I suppose I would. And that I was trying 'to dolly it up' a bit. I did a bit of a clean-up on board but do not know where to start with a refit. There is still a lot of gear and other treasures in the cabin.

I met the Winkle Picker on the way to Corraun. He was on his beat, beach combing. He says he checks the Corraun shore each day. I told him I had lost a bag and shoes and would pay to get them back. He said he'd 'spread the word'. His face, his clothes, his life, his intensity, his demeanor all seem like something right out of a Beckett play. I want to ask him if he will sit for a drawing but I guess he's a bit shy. Paul Henry had similar difficulty getting local people to sit for him.

We discuss the possibility of finding the body of one of the drowned shepherds on the beach.

He says one could get blown around Achill head and end up on the Corraun or Achillbeg shore. It seems unlikely to me.

Wednesday, January 19

It's a cold night and a calm clear day with a bit of sun. I checked the rocky beach and the gullies beyond it for bodies. I think it's a bit of a long shot that anything could end up on Achillbeg. A body would either have to come through the sound or, even less likely, around Achill Head against the prevailing winds.

Carving most of the day a 'Jonah and the Whale'. Confused, unsettled day. Went down for three loads of turf. Getting a bit fed up with the turf hauling duty, but what can you do? One more month should see the worst of the cold out. Three fishing boats left Cloghmore today heading out towards Achill Head. Perhaps there will be more EEC whiting.

Thursday, January 20

Art work all day. Did some work on the outboard motor in the evening. The outboard is the lifeline. Saw some sheep farmers in the island.

What is it about artists and islands? Possibly the most famous example is Paul Gauguin. Maybe he started the whole cult of artists being drawn to islands. He was a terrible man. Were he to do today what he did then he would have spent most of his life in prison.

The only Irish connection to Paul Gauguin seems to be Irish artist Roderic O'Conor from County Roscommon, who met Gauguin in Pont Aven in 1894, and at one point thought about going to Tahiti with Gauguin on his last, fateful journey to the South Seas. O'Conor, crucially, was present with Gauguin and two other artists and their girlfriends/models in the village of Concarneau when Gauguin had his famous brawl. His leg was badly injured. This injury was to cripple him him for the remainder of his short life.

Gauguin and his retinue were walking through the fishing village. They were a conspicuous bunch in a traditional, conservative setting. The local kids first jeered at the colourful band of bohemians, then started to throw stones at them. One of the kids got a slap from the artists and the row escalated to include the kids' fathers and the local fishermen, who resented the artists. Gauguin went down in the brawl and was brutally kicked and injured before things calmed down. Gauguin ended up in the local hospital with his shin bone sticking out of his leg and it never fully healed.

There are countless examples of artists on islands. Here in Ireland there is Paul Henry, Gerald Dillon, George Cambell. Synge went to the Aran islands, as did Seán Keating. The Blasket Island has its writers. Tory Island has its painting school thanks to Derek Hill.

Just to the south, poet Richard Murphy bought High Island, though he never tried to live there. He sailed out many times in his hooker to Inishbofin.

Richard Murphy also was sensitive about upsetting the local populace of Cleggan. He describes being called out of a pub for a fight over a poem he wrote. When Sylvia Plath had suggested to him that she cohabit with him in Cleggan for the winter he firmly declined her request, fearing it would incur the disapproval of the local people and the priest. At the time Plath was married to Murphy's friend Ted Hughes. Sylvia Plath returned to London. Shortly thereafter she killed herself.

Friday, January 21

I hauled the outboard down to the slip and tried using it. No good. So had to row over to Cloghmore and walk to Pattens for shopping and a visit to the post office. Had a good slagging match at the pub, joking about orgies in the island and the nudist colony over there. 'None of that with me,' I said.

Got a lift back with Jimmy who has a double-ended fishing boat about the same size as *Molly B.* Like many Achill islanders, he has a Birmingham accent.

The fishing boats at Cloghmore had a good two-day trip. The *Honey Bee* landed 60 boxes.

I got a nice witty letter from Tom, the younger brother, who is in school at Glenstal Abbey. It was composed in Latin. Very impressive. I am desperately trying to think up some Latin for a reply.

Saturday, January 22

Nice day. Light wind and sun had me stripped down to a t-shirt as I worked outside on the patio. I cleared all the bottles out of the ruin of a house to the west which I use for storage. I smashed them to smithereens in an orgy of aggression. I buried the lot under the patio. No rats are going to move in there.

Carving 'Jonah in the Whale', a sort of corny carving which features an image of Jonah carved in relief on the side of the whale. Or maybe it is magic realism. A good day's work. But feeling down at the world.

Perhaps I am listening to too much Radio na Gaeltachta and its sean nos singing. Some of it is very engrossing but sad. The singer would be in full flight and then suddenly stop and say, '*Go mo leis sceal*', clear their throat and then continue. Another time a nice female voice is singing away beautifully and I am transported to heaven but have not a clue what she is singing about. Then the English words 'Loyalist death squads' comes tumbling out as part of the song. Now that's a living art!

Sunday, January 23

Over to Dereens on a windy wet morning. Got a lift back with a young local lad who fishes on the *Border Prince*, another fine big ex-Scottish trawler. He's waiting for the cod fishing to start. He

also does some farming and told me that the lambs will be happening soon. He pointed out to me a deserted village which is on the slopes just above Cloghmore and which I had never noticed. The abandoned cottages quickly fade into the landscape. He pointed out a pattern of small fields which he said all used to be cultivated 'in my lifetime'.

Clean-up at the house and some work on the bowsprit of *Molly B*. I'm running low on wood to make things. Running low on everything, in particular money.

Wind increases over the day and it's presently blowing stink and raining.

Monday, January 24

S low-moving day. Up late (10.30) and somewhat depressed. Cold, windy and showery, some more work on patio. Hauled a bucket of coarse gravel from the rocky beach, hard work, there has to be a nearer supply.

It seems unlikely that John Lennon ever visited Achillbeg. But he did buy the adjoining island up the bay and had plans to live there. Imagine that! He should have asked my advice. The island he did buy, Dorinish, is no good for living on. I can see it across the bay in the distance when I look out my living room window. It's flat and exposed, a bit like a cartoon tropical island without the palm tree. The Beatles had a caravan delivered to the island. Then they came over to Ireland and stayed in the hotel in Mulranny. It was at the height of Beatlemania. They had a helicopter to ferry them around. That is how they got out to their new island. Presumably, they made a cup of tea in their caravan. The island is flat, windswept and low, barely hanging on against the onslaught of the Atlantic to the west. A typical drumlin formation like many of the islands in the bay. There are huge rounded erratic boulders everywhere but no rocky heights.

I landed on Dorinish once and had a look around, some ten years after the Beatles had departed, never to return. You could walk around the entire perimeter in less than ten minutes. It was a bit grim. A single field, a shale beach and a gentle slope up to a low cliff. There was little sign of even the hippies who had followed in the wake of the Beatles and who had made some attempt to inhabit Dorinish. They had spent more time in the pub at Westport Quay than they had on the island. The rats on the island were the main problem.

I was in Canada when John Lennon was shot dead in New York. I remember an excited Joss coming into my studio and telling me the news. The Canadian House of Parliament gave Lennon three minutes of silence at the behest of one of their liberal members. What an enlightened country!

Thirty years later an Egyptian/Irish businessman decided he would develop one of the other nearby islands. He poured vast amounts of money and energy into the project. He built guest houses, horse studs, recording studios, art studios, roads, jetties, sewage systems and utility buildings. He built an indoor heated swimming pool and Jacuzzi, a gym and games complex, a home cinema, and an outdoor sound system. He gave presentations, held seminars, hosted corporate development sessions. He launched CDs and whiskey brands. All on an island less than half the size of Achillbeg. He was trying to establish a brand, apparently – Innisturk Beg. And then he went bust.

I suppose that is what I was trying to do on Achillbeg – establish a brand. An art brand.

Tuesday, January 25

Up late. Under a cloud. Sometimes it's hard to keep pushing. There is no one to criticise or instruct. No one to admire the work. No one to provide motivation. No master to question or seek advice. No muse to inspire or impress. I could make a masterpiece here. Perhaps I did. And no one would see it.

I'm suffering from carver's wrist in my right hand, the result of using a heavy mallet for too long. I soaked the wrist in hot water and tried to rest it.

I walked around to the lighthouse side of island though it was windy and showery. I did some work on the tiller of *Molly B*, which has a Danish design carved on it copied from a book about the Vikings.

Wednesday, January 26

Another slow day. I changed my mind about crossing to Corraun to work on *Molly B* as the wind increased and there is a bad forecast, which proved correct. In spite of this, I saw *Honey Bee* going out fishing.

Thursday, January 27

I t blew a gale during the night but had eased off by morning. This allowed me to go over to Corraun by afternoon where I checked the boat and did the rounds. At the post office the postmistress was nice as is her husband. He has a 30-foot double-ender which he uses to bring sheep to Achillbeg where I had met him. We talked about conditions in the island. At the pub/shop – the Compass – I did some shopping. From the big picture window of the Compass there is a wonderful view of Achillbeg. Down at the boat shed there were sounds of work so I stuck my head in and asked if I could take a look.

They were working on an eighteen-foot boat which was half planked. Three other men were messing about with an old tractor. There was also an old yawl in there which I inspected. It's a well-equipped boat shed in need of a clean-up on the floor. I got the impression it is sort of rigged a bit to look busy. They admit that nothing much is happening in the boat-building department. 'We're waiting for the EEC.' Meaning that the EEC is expected to come up with some grants for the building of boats. I said I was sorry I could not order a boat and went and looked at another couple of yawls in the harbour.

On the *Molly B* I removed some bits which can be worked on in the house. Sort of homework. I waited till the top of the tide (6.00 p.m. and dark) to leave for Achillbeg.

For supper had a huge feed of bangers and mash and then prunes. I opened a five-pound tin of prunes, one of several I had bought 'on sale' in Panama as I was passing through on *Molly B*. I thought they were dried prunes, but they turned out to be sort of mushy and went moldy quickly in the heat of the tropics. So I kept this tin and hopefully the prunes will keep in the fridge as I munch my way through them.

Friday, January 28

Windy, wet day with gales forecast on the radio for Saturday. I did not bother with my normal trip out to Dereens, having done some shopping yesterday and not having any money. Well, I have £1.50 – not even enough for the bus fare to Westport.

There is an electricity blackout for about an hour. These blackouts happen quite frequently. They rarely last long and remind one how handy the ESB supply on the island is. In one sense the electricity is the most amazing and fortunate thing about Achillbeg Island. No question about it. It exists because of the lighthouse and was supplied to five houses on Achillbeg when the lighthouse was constructed in 1965. Ironically, as the electricity arrived, the people finally decided to leave Achillbeg.

The supply jumps the Blind Sound on high pylons. An attempt at an underwater supply failed. The tall line of poles stretches out across the breadth of the island to power the lighthouse. Branching off the lighthouse line, a spur feeds the houses. Even Clare Island at this time did not have a 24-hour electricity supply, as its houses were served by an intermittent generator.

The construction of the automated light in the years around 1963 to 1965 must have been a relatively busy time on Achillbeg. A tractor was brought over to the island to transport the building materials and the rough track it made as it hauled cement, sand and wood out to the site can still be traced on the island. This is the first record of a motorised vehicle on Achillbeg. Previously, the main form of transport would have been the donkey with either panniers or a cart.

The Achillbeg lighthouse is a modest structure, especially when compared to the light on Clare Island which it replaced. But it is an important navigational landmark guiding ships into Clew Bay and isolating Bills Rock as a danger. It is not really a tower in the traditional sense, but it has adequate height from the cliff on which it is built. One of the problems with the Clare Island light was that it was up too high and thus frequently obscured by mist.

When I first came to Achillbeg there was an odd set of lights, not unlike a traffic light, on Achillbeg. This was sighted on the brow of the hill on the road not far from my house. It was a signal light aimed at Cloghmore and Corraun to signal that the lighthouse, out on the far side of the island, was operating correctly. If there was a malfunction at the lighthouse then a red light would signal to the attendant watching from Corraun to investigate. Nowadays, there is an automatic radio monitoring signal in contact with the control center in Dun Laoghaire. Like a burglar alarm it warns the Keepers of the Lights if something is amiss.

Sometime after the installation of the lighthouse on Achillbeg the Commissioners of Irish Lights built a set of stairs in the cliffs below the lighthouse to maintain better access from the sea. This was a handy addition to the facilities on

Achillbeg, and is known as the Lighthouse Steps. It was from here that I tried in vain to fish for lobsters. When the Commissioners of Irish Lights go on their annual cruise of inspection around the Irish coast they use the Lighthouse Steps to land on Achillbeg.

More recently the Commissioners have added a helicopter pad at the site of the lighthouse and service it this way.

I have used the Achillbeg light extensively when sailing around Achill over the years. It has an ingenious system of white, red and green zones allowing the prudent navigator to avoid the nasty Bills Rock sitting out to the west. Long may the Achillbeg light shine in this day of GPS and electronic navigation devices.

Saturday, January 29

I moved back out to the main room to sleep. Too much noise in the back bedroom as the wind rattles the roof and rain hits the window. It blew stink most of the night but calms down a bit in the morning. The bar, from the Lighthouse Steps over to the rocky shelf at Corraun, was breaking. A mass of foaming water. It is the worst I have ever seen it. It's a combination of high swell and low tide, especially when the tide is ebbing and the wind at gale force. It would have been chancy for a 30-foot boat to go out or come in to the sound.

It's a day of work at an unexcited, steady pace. Some carving – another whale.

News on the radio that the three Achill farmers have been buried 'by a Bishop'. So they must have found the remains. Blowing, at times very violently, all day.

Sunday, January 30

Blew a gale all night. As strong as I can ever recall, I would think. It would be nice to have an anemometer. Slept badly in the main room. Cold. The breaking bar is even more impressive than yesterday. I fought the wind to walk down to the slip to check on the punt. It's OK. No question of going out of the island.

When the temperature gets below about six degrees it becomes difficult to get away from the fire.

Monday, January 31

Cold night on settee in the main room. Too lazy to do something about the bedding. I do believe it was milder outside the house than inside when I stuck my head out this morning. Windy and wet with some hail.

Working on my carving of the whale. I have never seen any whales in the waters about Achill. This is strange as there was a big whaling operation on the Inishkea Islands to the north of Achill in the early years of the last century, in the years before the First World War. This was established by a Norwegian company who used the techniques which they had perfected in the South Atlantic to hunt whales with steam whale chasers and explosive harpoons.

Where have all the whales gone? Where have all the basking sharks gone? Perhaps they can sense where they are not welcome.

Paul Henry, in his first book, has an amusing account of visiting the whaling station on Iniskea. He describes with much drama the smell and the mess of the whale-rendering works. The smell came from the rotting whales and the island was overrun by savage big pigs who fed on the offal. He found there a poitín distilling industry which then seemed to thrive on the islands. The crew of his hooker disappeared and got drunk and he had to round them up for the return journey. As the wind increased he had an exciting sail home to Achill as the crew slept it off.

Alexander Williams also deals with the fascinating subject of poitín or *uisce beatha*. He left a record in his journal about the drink. For some reason he wished to procure a quart. With his friend, Sheridan, they make a connection and score some from an old lady living in Dugort. She was obviously anxious to make a sale but also to stress the fact that she has nothing to do with the stuff. She brings Williams and Sheridan out to the potato patch. She digs around and 'finds' a keg from which the two lads decant a quart. Williams does not say how much the poitín costs but does mention that the bottle 'lasted for twenty years'. And it was powerful stuff. He seems to have maintained a supply to offer to guests.

Of course, everyone knows the place to get poitín nowadays is on Inishturk Island!

Chapter 11

An Paorach

And still they gaz'd and still the wonder grew,
That one small head could carry all he knew.
But past is all his fame. The very spot
Where many a time he triumph'd is forgot.
– Oliver Goldsmith

Tuesday, February 1

Up latish on cold windy morning. Not really a good idea to cross to the post office as I had hoped to do. I'm out of tea. And money.

Carving nice piece called 'West Wind'. I still have this carving. It's one of my favourites. Henry Moore was one of the first artists (and hopefully the last) that I consciously tried to copy. He had done a relief carving on a building in London called the 'West Wind' which I had admired and which is quite famous. My carving is quite different but I like to think that he gave me the idea. To carve, with a hammer and chisel, a depiction of the wind seems such a fantastic notion.

Wednesday, February 2

Wind eased off at last. Still cold. I take the opportunity to go over to Dereens where good load of mail awaits. Luckily there is some money awaiting me but no definite word about the Boat Show.

At the pier at Cloghmore, Joe the German was working on the *Honey Bee* which is gearing up for cod fishing. We looked at a catalogue which his artist friend Turi sent me from Austria. Turi paints big wall-sized paintings which are very complex, doodle-like abstractions. Sometimes a bit like Jackson Pollock. Here and there something representative will emerge such as a crocodile or a face, so there is a bit of levity, but by and large they are abstract. They are good and strong. Banks and big corporations buy them, apparently.

I sent Turi a business letter asking him to buy one of my works. He replied that he would but that he would like to see more of my work before making up his mind. And that was the last I heard from Turi.

Thursday, February 3

Clear, cold, sunny day. The sun brings out the work a bit, I do believe, enticing me away from the fire.

Saw the fox on the rocky beach picking at a very dilapidated piece of sheep carcass. He saw me after a few seconds and took off to the west towards the fort. I think it might be a different fox than Slim, the one I used to see before Christmas. Seemed smaller, a darker red and ran faster. I wasn't close enough to tell really.

The fishing fleet is out though there is a gale warning on the radio.

Friday, February 4

Up early (7.30 a.m.) keen to head up to Achill Sound in the punt but weather threatening and turned bad so changed my

mind. Rain and wind. A coffee-brewing day and reading rather than working.

Saturday, February 5

Still raining. Painting all day. Paintings with a marine theme for the Boat Show, perhaps.

If one seeks any indication of what a vibrant community existed on Achillbeg not so long ago, then surely it is the schoolhouse. It is directly across the valley from my front door.

Built in 1903, as the carved plaque above the door proclaims, it is a solid, tall, one-room structure. It dominates the central plain between the two mountain heights of the island. It has a well-built perimeter wall and an outside privy which has two cubicles, presumably one for the *caillini* and one for the *bucailli*. The standard of construction is excellent. Using cut stone and real slate for the roof it is far superior to the vernacular style of the other houses on Achillbeg. Inside there is a cut stone fireplace with a raised cast iron grate. There is a narrow hall section for storage and coat hanging. The large windows are the traditional school style, well above eye line, to prevent any distraction to the pupils. The interior wall sides are wood panelled. The floor is raised and timber, well ventilated from below. In front of the school is a fine area of flat grassland which was used as a football pitch. It was a National School.

When I first came to Achillbeg in the 1960s there were still old notebooks and a blackboard in the school. One could have held a class if one had pupils and a teacher. The two goal posts survived on the pitch in front of the school into the 1970s. The green painted front door of the school was still there into the 1980s. The fine Bangor slates on the roof started to go about the same time in the strong winds. The rain got in which caused the floor to rot. People, myself included, salvaged the timber as firewood. Today, all that is left are the four walls and the plaque proclaiming:

ACHILL BEG
NATIONAL SCHOOL
1903

The Office of Public Works once tried to sell the Achillbeg schoolhouse and advertised for tenders in the national press. I would have liked to buy it, save it and turn it into a studio. But a problem apparently arose with the title. It was taken off the market. Now it is a ruin, beyond reclamation.

Sunday, February 6

Too windy to cross to Cloghmore. The crossing might have been possible, and the wind calmed down over the day, but I thought it better to be prudent. Things like safety seem very relevant since the deaths of the three sheep men so recently. It would be easy for somebody to stop me living on my island by simply doing a 'job' on my boat. Stranger things have happened in these parts.

I turned the house next door into a rigging loft and laid out, on the floor, all the rigging from *Molly B* and started servicing it. It is galvanised iron wire, has seen a fair bit of service and so needs a certain amount of maintenance. A messy, black, tar-smeared, smelly job.

Monday, February 7

Sunny and cold. Light north wind. Carving in the morning and then over to Corraun, mainly to get some shopping and go to the post office, but also the diversion of visiting *Molly B*.

Ran into the skipper of the *Inish Arcan* again. He came aboard *Molly B* and sat around in the cabin in good form. Keen to chat and treat me as a fellow man of the sea. He complained about things in general, sang and recited Raftery:

> *Is Mise Raifteirí an file,*
> *Lán dúchais is grádh,*
> *Le súile gan solas,*
> *Le ciúnas gan crá.*

And so on. He tells me he had spent time in England in his youth but prefers it here in Corraun.

Tuesday, February 8

Bright sunny day with light northerly wind. Spent morning carving. I have started a carving called 'The Dream of Granuaile', which hopefully will be a major masterpiece.

I then succumbed to temptation to motor up to Achill Sound to do some shopping, the wind and tide being right for the outing. It's a mini-adventure. It was a nice run in the winter sun though a bit cold. There is snow on the mountains above, a definite snow line visible in the crisp clear conditions.

I did some shopping in Sweeney's then headed up to the paper shop, Bretts, where I was stopped by a man who introduced himself as Roddy Heron and he asked about Achillbeg. He said he lived near the graveyard at Kildavnet in Bleanaskill Lodge. He said that his sister was Hilary Heron (who I had heard of), the sculptor who married a man called Green in TCD (who I had never heard of). Hilary Heron was a contemporary of Oisin Kelly and both were now dead. They had visited and worked in Roddy's house. All this was quite a mouthful. But there was more. He was looking for five geese which had run away from his house, and indeed I had seen him using binoculars on the bridge. 'It's the foxes,' he said. No comment from me. He asked me what I was doing as if he already knew a certain amount about me. I told him I was painting, carving and writing. I don't think I mentioned forging in the smithy of my soul the uncreated conscience of my race. But if he had pressed me any further, I might have.

I offered to run him down the sound in the punt so he could look for his geese on the shoreline where they were likely to hide. He declined the offer.

We talked a bit about Achillbeg which he knows well. 'I'm the new wave,' I said, meaning the new wave of people going into Achillbeg. The 'new wave' was an expression then coming into vogue. Roddy took off in his car looking for his geese.

I ran out of money in Sweeney's and they gave me £10.00 credit. I'm using up all their supply of old doors and getting a lot of glass from them. It is the most famous hardware shop in Mayo and Joe Sweeney, the scion of the family, is famous for starting the Achill shark fishery. There was a bar behind the grocery shop in Sweeney's, and displayed there was one of the guns and a harpoon which might have come off the Norwegian whalers which used to operate out of the islands to the north.

It was a straightforward run back down the sound with the ebb tide. No sign of the fugitive geese. I stopped the motor opposite Roddy's house at Bleanaskill and drifted slowly by. There did not seem to be anyone there. I had admired the house many times; its remarkable assortment of trees and its location by the water makes it stand out.

Slight toothache and earache in the evening.

Wednesday, February 9

Ear cleared and was almost OK by morning. Calm, misty day. Seemed mild but thermometer in kitchen was reading much the same as ever. About five degrees. Today and yesterday are the first days in over a month when the fire has not completely dominated my existence. Supplying and feeding the beast and then sitting on top of it as it smolders away.

I journeyed up and down to the slip at least five times, bringing up things from the shopping spree yesterday. I also get started on a copper-and-tar patch to the punt where it is leaking. The punt, my lifeline to the outside world, is taking a battering on the rocky shores.

Much carving on 'Dream of Granuaile'.

Thursday, February 10

Cold. The Paorach, Francis Hugh Power, is probably the most powerful character associated with Achillbeg. If he had been on the Blasket Islands he would be as famous as Peig Seyers or Tomas O'Crohan. His house is known as the Paorach's house. He built it, apparently on commonage which is in itself a tribute to his standing with the islanders. It has a magnificent site on a flat plateau above and overlooking the beach. A real estate agent's dream. It had an upstairs loft, possibly the only house on the island to have such a thing, and has two distinctive small windows at second floor level in each gable. Perhaps that is where his guests stayed. I think it is the only house on the island which has a name that is widely known, The Paorach's House. The house is in ruins now. It was rented out to the Commissioners of Irish Lights as storage when they were building the lighthouse. I remember it being full of tarry barrels and bits of rope. The roof is gone. It was felted with tar rather than slated and did not last as well as slates might have.

The Paorach was the teacher in the Achillbeg school from 1913 to 1922. He was a big fan of the Irish language and culture, especially music. He could play the pipes and the violin.

He was instrumental in forming a music summer school on Achill and pupils traveled over to Achillbeg to his house on the island for lessons. He welcomed to the island future Nobel Prize winner and son of Maud Gonne, Sean McBride; future President of Ireland, Douglas Hyde; and, intriguingly, Peter Warlock, the English composer of the Capriole Suite. Among many others.

Warlock came to Ireland in 1917 to avoid the possibility of con-scription into the British army, then suffering horrendous casual-ties in France. He had lived happily in Wales and was interested in Celtic culture, particularly music. He was fond of collecting folk music, a popular pursuit for avant garde composers at the time. In this context he visited Achill in February 1918 and stayed for two months. He certainly was not a fair weather friend. He wrote about Achillbeg, 'I have never known such barrenness, such utter desola-tion', but he found the Irish language and culture there 'comprehen-sive and illuminating'.

Warlock met Yeats, the poet, and gave a talk on music in the Abbey Theatre in Dublin. He was fond of the drink and partying and was found dead in London in controversial circumstances in 1930, probably suicide. Bizarrely, the 'fruity' English art critic, Brian Sewell, claims to be the son of Warlock, being born in 1931, seven months after Warlock's death.

There does not seem to be any record of Warlock meeting Paul Henry, or indeed Paul Henry meeting the Paorach. But it seems pos-sible, especially as Henry became involved in amateur theatricals on Achill Island, something one might have expected to interest the Paorach.

The Paorach left Achillbeg and was promoted to a school in Newport in 1922. He ended his days in Galway, dying there in 1954, aged 75.

Friday, February 11

A good morning working at carving. The idea with the 'Dream of Granuaile' sculpture is simple. I carved a rectangular tower shape to the same proportions as Granuaile's tower at Kildavnet. Then, in relief, I carved on the four faces of the tower references to all the legends, stories and traditions I knew off or could find out about Granuaile. This was the sort of modus operandi which Geor-ganna often employed in her carving and drawing. She had a good line in Jungian gobbledygook to describe it, calling it the 'collective unconscious'. I used a lovely big piece of hardwood for the carving which I had picked up in the Panama Canal.

At the post office in Dereens I get good news from the Boat Show – they invite me to exhibit. I got all excited and rushed back to the house and started making frames. I would appear to have a slight shortage of suitable stuff to go into the frames but, not to worry. Pictures of radar reflectors perhaps.

Saturday, February 12

Walked out to the west to try to create some dramatic marine paintings, but low cloud obscured the vista. On a clear day there is a wonderful view of the Atlantic Drive and the shore line of Achill stretching all the way to Keem Bay from the west end of Achillbeg.

Sunday, February 13

Rowed over to Corraun to post letters and visit *Molly B*. At the harbour another boat was in, a 30-foot clinker double-ender from Purtin, 'down the island'. Strongly built, she was here for re-pairs having damaged her keel in Purtin harbour. Purtin harbour, on Achill Island, is a small maze of narrow compartments. It is exposed to the full force of the south west swells. No place to keep a boat in winter.

A couple of rough looking lads were aboard, hitting a complex piece of machinery with a hammer. Work boats around here have a hard time. I also spoke to the owner of the boat ahead of *Molly B* who was aboard. I told him I gave him a present of a fender but he did not take the hint that his boat is hitting mine. Worried about *Molly B* in that harbour, but will have to leave it until after the Boat Show.

Monday, February 14

It's cold. In a mad dash to get artwork finished and ready for the Boat Show. Up late carving and frame making. The varnish on the frames will not dry in the damp air.

Men in, rounding up the sheep and two big modern trawlers in at the pier. The trawlers go out together at dusk, pair trawling for herring.

Tuesday, February 15

Spent day leisurely packing for the Boat Show and carting stuff down to the slip. Getting ready to go. People would really appreciate these artworks if they knew the effort which goes into simply getting them to market.

Wind getting up from the southeast and hoping I am not cut off. The two pair trawlers from last night arrived back off the bar about midday, but decided not to enter on the ebb. They circled about the entrance all afternoon. Round and round they went waiting for the tide. It seems like a terrible waste of fuel to me, but these guys definitely know what they are doing. They went in at 4.00 p.m., at about half tide. I went up to the brow of the hill to watch them. They messed about a bit, veering across each other's bow, and then steamed in. Nice vivid sight. Oh, I do like workboats! They did not seem to have a big catch aboard for their night's work.

Wednesday, February 16

Crossed over to Cloghmore early with all my packages of artworks. There was much activity going on with the fishing fleet.

I tied the punt up afloat and asked Pádraig to look after it. Got a lift to the sound with the co-op manager in good time to catch the bus to Westport, and then the train to Dublin.

Chapter 12

The Rocky Road

One, two, three four, five,
Hunt the Hare and turn her down the rocky road
all the way to Dublin, Whack follol de rah!
– D.K. Gavan

My good friend Eddie English in Cobh just happened to be on the board of the organising committee of the Irish Boat show that year. He put in a good word for me so the Artist on the Island, who had just sailed solo across the Atlantic (not that common in those days), was invited to exhibit his pictures at the Boat Show in Dublin. It was not the Prado in Madrid or the Munich Pinakothek or the Rijksmuseum in Amsterdam, but what the heck – it got me out of my self-imposed exile.

The annual Boat Show in Dublin was then an important event. All the industry, such as it was, took stands and most people interested in sailing and boating would attend. But it was not the place for an aspiring modern artist or someone who thought he was the logical successor to Andy Warhol. That first boat show was a bit of a disaster. (I was to do many others in the coming years.) I had for exhibition mainly pages torn from notebooks made when making my voyage, framed elaborately in driftwood culled from the beach in

Achillbeg. I should have had pictures of yachts steaming downwind under spinnaker, or historical recreations of great moments in Irish yachting. The organisers were kind and indulgent and I made a few sales. (In later years, with more mainstream artwork, I had better success.)

I found it hard to drag myself back to my deserted island. I had a bit of an excuse to linger in Dublin. The dreaded Dutch elm disease was spreading through the land and the entire stock of elm trees in the country were dying. Elm makes reasonable carving wood and has a beautiful dark color and grain. There was an elm tree in my dad's garden that had died. I spent a few days salvaging wood for carving.

I took a walk down Grafton Street. There was Mick Mulcahy, the most famous artist in Ireland. He was sitting in a box using a vacuum cleaner to suck something out of the air. He was telling anyone and everyone in both official languages that he had given up drinking. Outside Bewleys, the Diceman was advertising something banal like double glazing or the Irish Permanent Building Society. There goes Phil Lynnot, tight jeans and Afro hair. There's someone from RTÉ. In the Bailey, the writers congregated and drank to excess. In the Coffee Inn was the only expresso machine in the country. In Nesbitts, revolution and smoke was in the air. 'Is that what it takes?' I wondered.

There were lots of vacant shops. 'I could just put my paintings there and sell them,' I thought.

U2, the rock group, were in the ascendance. I was of a slightly earlier generation. They were past busking in the Dandelion Market. I went to a poetry reading by beat poet Allen Ginsberg in Liberty Hall. There was an interval. I was moving seats in the crowded hall in the dark. I shuffled down along a line of seats. Suddenly I stumbled and accidently sat down in the lap of a scruffy looking fellow who was sitting with a group of friends. The friends grabbed me. I looked around to find I had sat down on Bono's lap. 'Oh hello,' I said and apologised. 'Hiya man,' said Bono. That was the only time I met U2.

Passing by the barber shop on Trinity Street I saw a striking young girl coming out. Jeans, t-shirt, doc's, midriff. And no hair. Just like Granuaile. She was bound for glory. Sinéad O'Connor.

My friend Dave came by with his cousin Ruth. A sensitive soul, she was interested in the island and the arts and my sojourn there. A few weeks later I received in the post a huge coffee table art book from Ruth. A beautiful guide to all the periods and styles from the Met Museum in New York. I think she was trying to educate me.

Dave and I had 'done' one of the first 'happenings' in Dublin. In protest at the censorship of the national TV station we had built a huge cage and put a TV set inside it. On the TV was a painting of a presenter who was gagged. Dave had made the TV and painted the picture. I had constructed the cage out of salvaged two by one pieces of wood. We left it on a grassy patch at the junction of the Stillorgan Road and Nutley Lane – the entrance to RTÉ. We called a newspaper seeking coverage but nothing happened. Somebody took our happening away. Maybe they censored the coverage of it!

It was nearly two weeks after the Boat Show that I headed west again to my island.

Wednesday, March 9

Caught the afternoon train to Westport. Once again it broke down somewhere around Athlone. I arrived too late to make a connection to Achill by bus. Getting to New York would have been quicker.

Thursday, March 10

I stayed overnight in Westport and bumped into Uncle Geoffrey who kindly offered to drop me to Achill after his work day ended. At 5.30 p.m. we set out, first collecting all my stockpile of luggage. This was a great help as my luggage included an outboard motor and heavy chunks of Dutch elm. At a windy Cloghmore we found the punt was damaged again. I decided to take Geoffrey's advice and stay on *Molly B* in Corraun for the night rather than cross over in the dark. He dropped me around to the little harbour there. I lit the stove and had a snug night in the comfy cabin of the *Molly B*.

Friday, March 11

Got under way from Corraun around 10.00 a.m. and hitched a lift from a postman to Achill Sound where I bumped into Roddy in Sweeney's hardware shop. Roddy ferried me to Cloghmore via Pattens pub. I am becoming a bit like a part of a pass-the-parcel game as I bounce around the locale.

I improvised a patch on the punt using debris from the shore, a cutting from a plastic bottle and a few nails. I rowed across reaching the house in the early afternoon. That's three days, door to door! All's well in the house but the punt needs a big repair. A new plank will have to be fitted.

Saturday, March 12

Letter writing. Some success with my mail order business. My old friends in Canada supported me, people who I had met on my travels bought stuff, friends and relatives helped me along. But the amounts of money were small. There was not really a living in it.

Sunday, March 13

I rowed across to Cloghmore and walked to Dereens. At the pub where I buy a paper there is a note from Roddy. He invites me over to his house this very Sunday for lunch. The bush telegraph is working.

Headed back to the island, getting a couple of nice pollock from the *Honey Bee* fishing boat on the way.

Got the overhauled outboard going and headed up the sound to Roddy's house. The motor started giving trouble at about Granuaile's castle so I abandoned the venture and went into Corraun. I rang Roddy from the pub there and made my excuses. Did some messing about on the boat and moved it away from the offending half-decker which is bumping the bow and whose owner is not too sympathetic. The harbour is a bit crowded. While *Molly B* is strongly built she is not up to bumping about each tide with a bunch of workboats from the west of Ireland. I tied up outside the *Inish Arcan*, which is also not ideal as she has a much bigger, deeper hull than that of *Molly B*. Boats are happiest when they are the same size tied up together.

Got back to the house about 7.30 p.m., tired. There is a big fishing fleet at Cloghmore and the word is that the cod season has been good.

Sent a letter to the Galway Arts Festival telling them they need me.

Monday, March 14

A reasonable work day, painting all morning. Oil painting and building an easel. Down to the slip in the afternoon. It's sunny weather so good opportunity to work on the punt. I put a better copper patch on the bilge of the punt. My boat is like an old pair of shoes which need to be re-soled.

The Winkle Picker was in to Achillbeg again but did not land at the slip. I gave him an old Seagull outboard motor (which I could not start) the other day and told him I had some spares for it at the house which he could have. I think he might be avoiding me, but perhaps I am just being paranoid.

Tuesday, March 15

A bad, slow day. Did some painting but not that happy with it. Oil paintings of sharks and whales and Clew Bay. Took about three hours to get the fire going with damp firewood and turf.

I was standing outside the open front door chopping firewood when there was a whiz and a bang. Something flew in the front door and crashed into the pane of clear glass forming the window of the porch opposite the door. It fell to the ground. I rushed in, threw a towel over it and picked it up. It was some kind of small falcon or hawk or other bird of prey and badly shook up. It was about the size of a blackbird. I held it for a while and had a good look. Very beautiful with its green/yellow plumage and sharp hooked beak. Gradually it revived and after about five minutes I could hoist it up in the air and release it. That is the only time I have seen a bird of prey on Achillbeg. Achill is well known as a habitat for eagles in days gone by and the name Achill may even be derived from that connection. The eagles are reputed to have largely died out about the mid-nineteenth century. Sea eagles survived in the locale up to the end of the century.

The most inspiring bird on Achill is surely the wren. They live in the walls in their tiny micro-environments. It must be difficult for them to avoid the rats, especially at nesting time.

Wednesday, March 16

Another slow day. Foggy, damp and mild. The sheep are producing lambs all over the island, a fine, amusing sight. However, one of them gives birth to an injured, stillborn lamb, in the shelter of the east gable of the house. I could see the entire painful episode right outside the window. I thought the mother was going to die but she walked off nonchalantly leaving an awful mess behind her which I hope the foxes remove tonight.

Thursday, March 17

St Patrick's Day. Foggy and some wind. I wonder how they celebrate Paddy's Day beyond in Achill.

The new lambs are much in evidence, hopping about like wind-up toys in their shiny new coats. Full of the joys of life. The whole island is a cacophony of bleating. The lamb bleats, the mother replies. The mother bleats, the lamb replies. Like a radar system or a bunch of fog horns. The mother keeps on grazing. That's what sheep do most of the time. The new-born lamb explores its new, fascinating world, intermittently dashing back to base to have a feed from the patient mother. There are many twins, the occasional triplets.

The black ones stand out. As I say repeatedly, 'Achillbeg would be a lonely place without the sheep'.

The stillborn lamb's remains at the east gable end of the house moved about three meters during the night and was much picked at. Disgusting sight. I picked it up with a stick and threw it down at the bottom of the hill away from the house. Later in the morning I noticed a big black bird pecking at it. A rook or raven. Half an hour later it seemed to be gone completely. Perhaps the fox…

Friday, March 18

Wet and foggy with light wind from the west. Letter writing and then over to the post office at Dereens. I had to walk from, and back to, Cloghmore. No lift. It's the first time in ages I haven't been picked up and given a lift by someone.

Big load of mail at the PO. One letter from the Arts Council officer in Galway who, it would appear, does not have much to put in her arts guide for May/June for the Achill region. She asks me to supply news of arts events in the region. Almost appointing me as her agent! No art events in the region? How surprising! I'll have to see if I can rustle up something for her to print in her calendar.

Saturday, March 19

More fog. Painting pictures of sharks. It's rare to see a shark around Achillbeg but Achill has many associations with sharks. It is a popular spot for shark angling and the basking shark fishery centred on Keem Bay is famous. It was while scuba diving at Keem bay that I saw a basking shark underwater and got quite a fright. But the shark turned out to be dead, tethered to a cliff and awaiting collection by someone. Further down the coast I bumped into another shark, a smaller one this time. I was with two other divers and it moved across our line of vision about ten meters ahead. We panicked and got out of the water pronto. There we met a group

of more experienced divers who immediately jumped in to have a look. They could not believe how fortunate we were to have seen such a sight.

The basking shark fishery existed in Achill from about 1950 until it ceased around 1970 as the supply of sharks dramatically tailed off. At its height over 1,000 basking sharks could be killed in a year. They were netted and then killed from a currach with a harpoon. The liver was reduced for its oil. Remains of the boilers and tanks used in the shark fishery are still visible at Purteen harbour on Achill Island.

My shark paintings were small watercolours. I was interested in the conventional view of the shark. Shark as predator, killer, king-pin. A wonderful, passionate, subject. Damian Hirst, who took up the subject some ten years later to dramatic effect, went all the way to Australia to find the first shark he pickled.

Sunday, March 20

Up early (7.30) and carving. But carving of Granuaile's Dream is not to my liking. I had hoped it would turn out better. It is very detailed, cluttered and fussy. It's less sculptural and more graphic.

Over in the punt to Cloghmore. I stopped at the post office at Dereens and I got another little note from Roddy inviting me over that day for lunch. So I arrived at Roddy's fine Bleanaskill Lodge and had a very enjoyable day with him. He cooked a fine piece of cod with spuds on his Aga and we ate in his comfy living room overlooking the sound. The tide coming and going in front of his living room marked the hours. The dark purple mountains of Corraun were a wonderful backdrop on the other side of the water.

We talked of the sea and Achill and, of all things, art. His very nice collection of paintings, mainly centred on his late sister's friends, is refreshing to see in this part of the world. In particular, he had a couple of very fine, early Hilary Heron carvings. These were of disgruntled Irish characters with their hands in their pockets. As Roddy explained, 'They're all messed up'.

Roddy showed me Hilary's photos and scrapbooks. She had a great collection of Bovril bottles found by digging in dumps. Many postcards and illustrations of Picasso works carefully mounted in albums. Looking at them you could see how difficult it was, not that long ago, to get illustrations of modern or indeed any art.

Roddy seemed to like the pictures of Basil Blackshaw, which I don't much care for. He had several. He talked about Alexander Williams who had owned and largely built the house in which we sat, and who had planted the garden. I was a bit embarrassed not to have heard, at that stage, of Williams in whose house I was sitting.

In the afternoon we drive over to Corraun in his car, he to see some land he says he wants to buy and me to check on *Molly B*. He is interested in *Molly B* but I think is also welcome of the excuse to see his land without being seen by the locals to be snooping about. *Molly B* is in a bad position relative to the boat next door. I will have to do something about it.

Roddy tells many interesting tales of Achill and his tribe (the Anglo Irish) and the Achill people. He fished commercially in the old days when there were no doghouses on 50-foot trawlers and they had to winch the net in by hand. He has bad arthritis, especially in his hands, he complains. He holds up a powerful, gnarled, bony clenched fist to show me. He attributes the arthritis to the time he spent hand winching on fishing boats.

I mentioned Mrs. Boydell to Roddy. He was not a big fan. 'She came walking in here with that friend of hers,' he said in an irritated voice. (Mrs Boydell often brought a companion to the island.) 'And why shouldn't she?' I asked. We joked about his stand-offishness and I said, 'Yes, she had the audacity to say hello to me when we met over on Achillbeg!'

In the late afternoon he dropped me back to the pier at Cloghmore. He asked to buy a picture 'of a boat'. I said I would get one for him. (He bought a picture of a currach.) I bailed out the punt and headed home.

Monday, March 21

Bad forecast on the radio. It blew all night and prevents trip to Corraun to do something about *Molly B* which is damaging itself against a trawler. Cold and crouched over fire all day reading Viney's new book of collected articles from *The Irish Times*.

Tuesday, March 22

Still blowing a bit in the morning but not enough to prevent me hopping over to Cloghmore. But bad enough to make Corraun out of reasonable reach. Wind eases off over the day. Walk over to

rocky beach and then over the top of the north hill of Achillbeg and down to the slip. A very good view of Achill Sound from up there.

Wednesday, March 23

Cold, windy, wet. Weather still too bad to permit planned trip over to Corraun.

Granuaile, Grace O'Malley, Grainne ne Maile, Granny Imallye, the Pirate Queen, however you want to call her, permeates the land. I am at the centre of her kingdom which were the shores and islands of Clew Bay. Achillbeg guards the entrance to Kildavnet castle and the pool below it. Many call it Granuaile's castle. Three miles away is her fortress on Clare Island. Up the coast is the fine tower house at Carraigahowley, also called Rockfleet. This she grabbed from her second husband, Richard Bourke, when she cast him out, keeping their son and citing Brehon law.

As an Irish icon, Granuaile takes some beating. Straight from central casting she has come down to us as a pirate queen, a feminist hero and an enduring historical personality from the Celtic mists. That she existed there is no doubt. This is not Finn Mac Cool or Leopold Bloom. I had first read of her in Eleanor Fairburn's historical novel *White Seahorse*. Now I rushed out and bought the recently published Anne Chambers biography.

The documentary evidence survives in archives and libraries. She has inspired writers, composers, lyricists, legends and myths, Broadway plays and marketing campaigns. What other female from that period has survived as a personality in the popular imagination to such an extent?

This was the time of the Earls, the plantations, 'surrender and re grant', the start of the 'wild geese' and the period leading up to the Battle of Kinsale. Granuaile did not take any part in that conflict. In true pirate fashion she was mainly interested in protecting her own territory. She probably had no concept of Ireland as a nation. More likely, she was interested in her own family lands and its position

within a Celtic culture stretching from Scotland south to the Iberian Peninsula. These tribal groupings spent their time forming and breaking alliances with each other. And stealing each other's cattle.

The outside enemy was the Sassenachs who were trying to impose their rules and customs over Granuaile's territory. Imposts, or custom duties, were the main source of income which a ruler had in those days. There was little taxation. A lord provided armies for his king. He got men and food from his tenants. Income was provided by levying taxes on imports of goods. For this reason, Galway was the most important city on the west coast. Granuaile, with her pirate galleys lurking to the north, safe in their island harbours, was in an excellent position to pounce.

Did she cut off her hair, Sinéad O'Connor fashion, and with much the same results, to enable her to go to sea as a young girl? I would think so. Could she predict the weather? Probably. Did she kidnap the heir to Howth Castle and hold him to ransom? Possibly. Did she kill 100 Spanish survivors who might have been cast up on the shores of Clare Island? Apparently so. These were tough times and the Spaniards might have been misunderstood and have tried to take boats. Did she give birth to her son Tibbot ne Long on a galley while it was being attacked by Turkish invaders? Did she then rise from her bed, post-birth, and rally her men to repel the boarders? Seems unlikely.

That she stood on Achillbeg must be certain. The beach and anchorage here would have been highly important to the boats of the period entering the sound. Proof of this can be found on many ancient charts of the sixteenth century. Achillbeg is frequently noted as prominent as Achill itself. It would have been O'Malley territory and as important and as secure as the harbour on Clare Island.

Following an exciting life which immortalised her, she probably retired to her island origins. Nobody knows for certain where she died. I would like to think of her living out her final days overlooking the harbour on Clare Island. There she would stroll down to greet any new ship docking in the harbour and seek news of the turbulent world outside. The same question which islanders used to ask Synge three hundred years later: 'Is there any war in the world at this time, a *duine usala*?' A world in which she once played an important part.

By tradition, she is buried in the Abbey on Clare Island.

Am I related to Granuaile? Most of the population of Mayo make such a claim, so why not?

Thursday, March 24

S unny, showery, windy day. Boat work. Working on solid wooden masts of *Molly B*, filling the extensive cracks in them with tar. Messy business. The house is stinking of tar and my hands are ruined.

Saw the fox, just a glimpse out to the west where some seagulls were squalling at him for some reason. (Seagulls can be very territorial.) I went to get the binoculars but the fox was gone. Also ravens in evidence soaring and making nice noises. Must be good feeding season for them with the sheep and lambs.

Friday, March 25

B lustery wet and cold. I deemed it wise not to go out to Dereens as I usually do on Friday. Reading in front of the fire.

Dipping into Bruce Arnold's book on Irish art. He quotes the famous line, which Jack Yeats exclaimed, about the modernists and cubists: 'Who the blazes is Gleizes?' This prompted me to write some doggerel on the page of a sketch book:

> *Who the blazes is Gleizes,*
> *What's the use of Mabuse.*
> *Ham fisted fellow was Donatello,*
> *And not much surer was Albricht Durer.*
> *Who the hell was Bruegel*
> *What the heck is Lautrec.*
> *Much too far went Auguste Renoir*
> *And a miss give Matisse.*

For a queer was Vermeer
(He was pally with Dali),
Just as grotty was Buonarroti
And very poor is Henry Moore.

Saturday, March 26

Got out to post office early in a lull in the weather. Lots of important news. I am to be presented with an award by the yacht club in Dublin for my voyage from Vancouver to Ireland. That will be next month. It is with a little too much glee I greet this news – another chance to get away from Alcatraz.

But there is more. Big news at the post office is that Neil, the brother, and Nora are to get married next week! Nora is from, where else, but Westport! They ask me to be best man. That means I have to get up to Dublin next Tuesday.

Over to Corraun in the afternoon to do a clean-up on *Molly B* and some shopping. Long chat with Sweeney from the pier. A nice calm man and apparently the pier is called after him by the locals. 'Sweeney's Pier'. He is nice and direct and asked me, 'Are ye a painter by trade?'

'No,' I said, hesitatingly, 'I'm a painter by process of elimination.' Meaning, I suppose, that I had tried everything else.

Sunday, March 27

Nice day, with clocks changing. Summer time. Another milestone passed. The days are spreading, the temperature rising. Growth starts. The island changes colour from the sepia reds to hints of emerald greens.

I walk out to the lighthouse. I can do some meditation. I feel that I have done enough wandering on the mainland side yesterday. Saw and stalked the fox out by the lighthouse. It did not see me coming.

I think its lair is there. Seems to be in good looking shape with red shiny coat. It noticed me and fled.

There is a fantastic view of Clare Island from the lighthouse on Achillbeg. Two miles across the open Atlantic rises the sheer cliffs of the west side of the island, soaring up to the heights of Knockmore some 460 meters above the sea and the breaking reefs below. It's perhaps the best view of Clare Island one can get.

The dramatic location of the old lighthouse on Clare is in the foreground perched on its own plateau. It is an extensive compound of two towers, keepers' cottages, out-buildings and a large perimeter wall, all whitewashed. It is clearly visible against the dark blue rock of the cliffs as was the intention. The waves break incessantly on the Croaghan Rocks 200 feet below. There is quite a contrast with the simple low tower and the unmanned light on the Achillbeg side.

Below the Achilbeg light is a large off-lying reef of rock where a colony of cormorants drying their wings can be seen. They are there now. This sight always reminds me of Flannan Isle and the poem which I had to learn at school. The three lighthouse keepers disappear and the poet brilliantly suggests that they have been trans-formed into cormorants.

Monday, March 28

Busy day of mainly boat work. Painting and oiling mast and spars. Having filled all the many cracks in the masts with tar I now give it a coat of linseed oil. Terrible mess in the house from tar, solvents and tools. A grown mast is a living thing with its 'checks' (rather than cracks). The masts have dried out over the winter, being indoors, so the checks have opened up, like a pine cone predicting fine weather. Filling them with tar seems like a reasonable thing to do. The tar will stay pliable and prevent moisture from penetrating. I squeeze the roofing tar into the checks and scrape off the excess with a spatula.

I make preparations for leaving on the morrow. I have nothing to wear to a society wedding in Dublin! And me the best man!

At midday the big trawler, *Border Prince*, runs aground on the bar at low water while trying to go out to sea. There were big swells rolling in. She reversed off and went back to Cloghmore. First time I've ever seen any boat in difficulties on the bar.

Tuesday, March 29

Departed early, before 7.30, to get to sound for the 9.00 a.m. bus. Luckily got a lift and also connected with another lift from Westport to Dublin.

The wedding of the brother, Neil, to the fair Nora from Westport is a suitably grand and important affair. As best man I have very little to do as the entire proceedings unfold without a hitch.

Again, the city holds me in its grip. Easter is happening shortly. I decide to stay on in Dublin for a few days.

I start to take an interest in the city and its history. I start to paint and draw it. I make a pilgrimage to the Joyce landmarks, the Martello tower, Sandymount strand and the Bailey pub where the number 7, Eccles street door was still then on display.

I had found Joyce's works difficult and boring. But his life story, his struggle and his travails, triumphs, tragedies and wiles I found fascinating. From Ellmann's celebrated biography, to the revealing letters, to other accounts of his peripatetic life and relationships with others, I could only admire the famous Irishman.

Joyce himself was an island. He liked big cities and sophisticated company, grand hotels and *chi chi* restaurants. He would not have come near Achill to save his life. But he had few friends. He used people. Though a modernist writer he had little time for modernist painting. 'Get my tie straight,' he said to one of his portraitists, Patrick Tuohy. My favorite quote from him, which he repeated in letters, was that he had no imagination. 'My head is full of pebbles and rubbish and broken matches and bits of glass,' he said to his patron,

Miss Weaver. He could write sitting in an armchair surrounded by mayhem, paper on his knee, Nora, visitors and the children in the same room, creditors beating down the door, doctors removing chunks of his eyes, the Nazis just over the horizon. Is that a definition of insular?

Chapter 13

The Days Will Grow Longer

Anois teacht an Earraigh
beidh an lá dúl chun shíneadh,
Is tar eis na féil Bríde
ardóigh mé mo sheol.
Go Coillte Mach rachad
ní stopfaidh me choíche

Now with the springtime
The days will grow longer
And after St. Bride's day
My sail I'll let go
I put my mind to it,
And I never will linger
– Raftery

Saturday, April 9

I headed back to my island fortress. The trip back from Dublin in-volved a lift with Clare to Tinahely, County Wicklow. Then a transfer to Mary Clare's car which brought me to Westport. I spent a half day lolling around Westport and then caught a bus to Achill

Sound. From there I walked and hitched to Cloghmore. More pass-the-parcel stuff. One and a half days, door-to-door.

Bought some nice cod from the fish co-op at the sound.

Sunday, April 10

S trong wind from the northeast, an unusual direction. Re-arranged house a bit and moved masts outside. Crossed all the way over to Dereens in the afternoon to post a letter. But forgot to bring a stamp.

Monday, April 11

M ade good push on getting masts ready to go sailing. I move them back inside and glue them with better sheave arrangements. Also glued the oar.

The oar is a very important part of *Molly B*'s equipment. It's a single sculling oar about fifteen feet long. A bit like those used by a Venetian gondolier. It does not really push the six-ton *Molly B* very far but is essential in light winds for swinging the stern around to face the hull in a new direction. It's not really warm enough for glue but I have to get on with it. Using the electric heater.

Headed over to Corraun harbour in afternoon to cook some rashers aboard *Molly B*. She has been badly damaged on her topsides by the trawler she's tied to. The trawler was using a big balk of wood as a fender and that started sawing its way through the hull of *Molly B*. Not good.

Tuesday, April 12

C ool, calm, sunny day. Work on masts, moving them outside again now that the glue has set. For good this time, so freeing up some space inside the living room.

Wednesday, April 13

It's my birthday. Well, I don't usually bother with that anymore. Productive day both with boat preparation and carving. I am carving a nice block-shaped piece called 'St Patrick and the Snake'. It was suggested by the block of wood which I had, a massive piece of Lignum Vitae which I got somewhere in Central America. There is relatively little carving to do. One cannot easily carve Lignum Vitae anyway because it is so dense and sinewy. It's more a sort of careful drilling and cutting operation.

Lignum Vitae is an interesting wood used extensively on sailing ships and many other places in days gone by. It is incredibly heavy, hard and dense, so much so that machine parts were made out of it. It does not float. Bits of Harrison's famous chronometers were made out of it. Several of my carving mallets are made of it.

The temperature is in the range 12 to 15 degrees. Positively balmy. One thinks back with horror to the distant, dismal, bad old days when I sat crouched over the fire all day.

Thursday, April 14

Back to cold again. Slow day. Varnishing boat items and carving. Working on the rigging in the house next door.

I walked over to the fort in the afternoon checking the rocky beach on the way. The Iron Age fort is a bit of an enigma. Dun Kilmore it is called. It is one of the most important promontory forts on the west coast of Ireland. Save for one in Dingle it is described as

'the most complex of the Irish promontory forts' by T.J. Westropp who surveyed it in 1910. It is quite understated and subtle on first inspection. It is easy to miss it when you first explore the island. But on closer examination it grows on you and you begin to realise you are somewhere special.

It is a wonderful place to visit. Inspiring. The site and the evidence of ancient occupation put the nearby Céide Fields to shame. There can be no doubts about Dun Kilmore and it has never been excavated.

Who were these people who could live in such extreme places? Perhaps the climate was more benign. Possibly the defensive nature of the site was all important. Who was the enemy?

To sit overlooking the fort and see the Atlantic breaking on three sides, Clare Island in the distance and the jagged cliffs of Achill to the other side produces the most wonderful feeling of awe. There is some suggestion that a round tower once occupied the site. This is likely to have been a later Christian addition. Like the monastic remains on High Island and the Scelligs rocks to the south, Achillbeg may have been a monastic outpost following its Iron Age existence.

Friday, April 15

Breezy morning put plans for an early run up to Achill Sound astray. Up late and reading *The Moon and Sixpence*, Somerset Maugham's book based on the life of Paul Gauguin. Maugham arrived in Tahiti in 1916 to research his book. He was lucky to be there early enough to buy a door which Gauguin had decorated in a house which he, Gauguin, had rented. Maugham bought it for the price of a replacement door and ended up bequeathing it to the Tate Gallery in London. He was followed by many others who beat a hasty charge to Tahiti and the Marquesas Islands in search of Gauguin's works which might be overlooked and cheap. Paul Gauguin's possessions after he died were auctioned off by a receiver to pay his debts on the islands. There was little interest in the paintings, carvings tools and other artifacts which he left behind. The unsold lots were burned. He is buried on the Marquesas Islands. It was his friends back in France, and the fact that he had written a wonderful memoir, that caused collectors and curators to take an interest in his work. His reputation blossomed.

He left at least two children on the islands and one of them was discovered by a female American tourist and encouraged to paint. She marketed his works all over the world. She brought him to America where he stayed painting and trading on his name for the rest of his days. Gauguin's legitimate children in Denmark largely rejected him. One daughter, to whom he was close, died tragically young.

Rowed with wind and tide over to Corraun Harbour in late afternoon, being out of petrol which had siphoned out of the tank. Got petrol and rang Pattens to see if there were any messages for me. Maybe people coming for the weekend. None. Hang about boat for a while getting depressed about further damage from trawler and the prospect of re-rigging it in that desolate harbour. Returned to the slip at the top of the tide, the wind getting up from the southwest.

Saturday, April 16

Slow day mentally, getting a bit impatient with Achillbeg. It's difficult to stick with it. Nothing much on the horizon. No one is going to discover the Artist on the Island. 'If you want to get up, you got to get out' is a saying well known in Achill. Paul Henry moved to Dublin. To conquer the world Joyce had to be in Paris. Warhol moved from the slums of Pittsburg to New York. Granted, Gauguin stayed in the islands. But it was well after he died that anyone came looking for him.

Got much carving done, however, on 'Dream of Granuaile'. It is nearly finished but looks a bit overdone, a bit too finicky, I would

think. It's more a narrative relief carving and less a piece of sculpture.

It's possible to carve when depressed, I find. Indeed, it's probably a good antidote. The physical act takes over. The noise creates an internal world, maybe like listening to music on earphones. The mind settles down, the chips fly, a rhythm sets in. There's an area that needs to be roughed out. You change one thing, you have to change another. As you are changing that, you notice something else. You have to change everything. And so on it goes. You always obliterate what you don't like. The hours pass. Then you look at it one day and it's finished.

Cold, April, showery day. It's the best time of year to see the massed Paul Henry cloud formations over the purple hills and reflecting water.

Sunday, April 17

Vincent delivers some wood to Cloghmore to me but I miss meeting him. Nice to get some encouragement.

Spent the day dreaming up great sculptural projects to be built upon the island. Among them a giant 3 and a floating 'I'. A spiral maze and an earthwork shark. I don't know how many of them will get built. The plans will never get further than my notebook.

Monday, April 18

Up early on a clear frosty morning. I'm painting and decorating in the house, mainly in the kitchen and bathroom. Trying to get rid of grunge. I want to leave the house in some sort of reasonable condition.

Tuesday, April 19

Cold, sunny, fresh, northerly wind. The north wind makes it difficult to head up to Achill Sound village. But I am out of many things. The cupboard is bare, so I head off. The tides are favourable, it's two hours before the top. The strong north wind means a pronounced 'wind against tide' effect in the channel where the current is strong. I simply hold the bow of the punt into the wind and the tide pushes me up to Achill Sound. Both the wind and tide will flush me back to my island on the ebb.

Bought, among other things, a lobster pot and a bag of cement. A bag of cement was a heavy item in those days before the EC regulated its size. It makes sense to transport it by boat from the Sound to the beach on the island in one operation. Then wheelbarrow it to the house by the shortest overland route.

Nice run back down the sound with wind and the ebb tide pushing me along. I rounded Darby's Point in fine style and rode the eddies all the way out to the beach at Achillbeg.

Saw a lamb which had been born without any woolly coat. Weird sight. It runs madly about and does not last long without insulation. The rooks move in for the pickings.

Set the new lobster pot at Lighthouse Steps using an old dried cod head for bait.

Wednesday, April 20

Up and over to the lobster pot on a sunny cold morning to find one small edible crab. It's always easier to get up out of bed if one has a lobster pot to check. I cooked and ate the crab.

Headed over to Corraun Harbour for work on *Molly B.* Another yacht has arrived into the harbour, the only other sailing boat in the area if you do not count the local yawls.

Bought a fish from a trawler at Cloghmore, a nice big ling for £1.00. I set the lobster pot with the head of the ling. It has been a gastronomic day:

Breakfast: Crab, cereal, pancakes and tinned ham, tea, grapefruit, apple.

Snack: Tea, cold cuts, cheese on bread.

Lunch: Cod, bread, tea, apple.

Dinner: Pork chop, spinach, tomato and mushroom salad, cheese, yogurt and coffee.

Thursday, April 21

One edible crab in pot. I removed the claws and throw the rest away. It's too much hassle to cook a whole crab. It stinks up the entire house with fishy steam and uses up loads of gas. Then there is not much eating on the body of the crab.

Got the 'Dream of Granuaile' off the pedestal though it's not finished and never will be. Unfortunately, I do not have a photo of this piece. It was sold through Kennys Gallery in Galway. (If you happen to own it I would appreciate hearing from you.) The illustration in this book is an approximation of the imagery involved.

Friday, April 22

I have to get to Dublin this weekend to be presented with a prize. Windy, wet day, but over to Corraun anyway, mainly to buy petrol for the outboard. Met Denis Gallagher, the local T.D. and Minister of State who lives close to the harbour. He was a bit guarded as he shook my hand as if trying to figure out what way I would vote. It's impressive that a man from Corraun gets to be a T.D. and Minister in the competitive maelstrom of Mayo and national politics.

Built a fire in *Molly B*'s stove and waited around hoping for the weather to ease. Which it did not. Motored over to the castle at Kildavnet, Granuaile's castle, and walked to the post office.

My favorite story about Granuaile is that she used to tie the rope from her galley to her bed post. Sometime the story is that she tied the rope to her foot when she slept. It certainly would be possible at Kildavnet castle, or the tower at Rockfleet (Carraigahowley), as the tide comes right up to the base of each tower. Presumably, she did this so that no one could steal the galley. Other versions of the story claim that it is to know when the tide returns. A sort of middle ages alarm clock. I had to, of course, include this story in my carving so there is a rope running all over the piece.

The Dream. Of Grannuaile.

Pete Hogan.

Back at Cloghmore pier I made enquiries about the possibility of a lift on a fish truck to Dublin which I was told might be possible.

I went back to the house, dried out, packed a bag and returned to the pier to find that the truck goes to Galway only. There is a national bus strike, a common enough occurrence in those days. Like Georganna some months ago, I am desperate to get out of here!

I toyed with the possibility of heading across the bay to Westport in the 14-foot punt. Prudence got the better of me however. That is certainly the sort of stunt to upset the local people. In any case, the weather is not suitable for such a trip. But I must get to Dublin.

Saturday, April 23

Got an early start and a lift from Cloghmore to Achill Sound. Then my luck failed. I walked the whole way to Mulranny, hitching. No lifts. It's a 10-mile walk parallel to the abandoned train line. Then a truck collecting garbage picked me up. I was very grateful as we stopped to collect all the garbage between Newport and Castlebar. But I was in time to catch the train to Dublin and a place on the top table.

In a slap-up dinner the Royal St. George Yacht Club presents me with an award for sailing from Vancouver to Ireland, engineless, in *Molly B*. The award trophy was the last sextant that the famous Bill Tilman had used on his voyages, mounted on a plaque. (Tilman and the crew of the sailing tug *En Avant* had been lost at sea while on an expedition to the Antarctic.)

On this visit to Dublin I manage to avoid the pitfalls and flesh-pots of the big city and head back to my island almost immediately. This time the train does not break down, the bus crews are back working and I don't miss any connections. Ten and a half hours door to door. That might stand as a record.

Wednesday, April 27

Crossing over to the island I find 'POISON LAID HERE' signs all over the island – at the slip, outside the house and at the Lighthouse Steps. I presume it might be some legal requirement when you put down poison for foxes. But I cannot help being annoyed at it. I have never seen such signs on the island before.

At the Lighthouse Steps the lobster pot which I had left in the water is gone. That's not very friendly. Fishing a lobster pot by throwing it in from the shore is not going to impact on the local fishing industry.

I feel a bit like Robinson Crusoe when he finds a footprint in the sand. There's something going on. Perhaps it's a bit more like that more pessimistic book in the genre – *Lord of the Flies*.

My first island book was the famous *Coral Island* written by Scottish writer R. M. Ballantyne in 1857. It was one of the first books I had ever read and I suppose I thoroughly approved of the Victorian, colonial sentiments therein portrayed. I have never been able to read the original *Robinson Crusoe* from cover to cover, having tried several times. A book which should be in the genre but is probably forgotten is *Brown on Resolution* by my favorite author of all time, C.S. Forrester. Brown, with his trusty Lee Enfield rifle, on a desert island, sacrifices himself as he delays the German Navy raider long enough for it to be destroyed by the pursuing British.

Thursday, April 28

Less troubled today by poison signs. I presume they are there to eradicate the foxes. I presume it is the law of the land. I keep busy. I go over to Corraun to check on *Molly B*. I worry about her over there. She's OK. I had to use the nine-foot tender to get there as I discover a hole in the punt. It has dried out on a sharp rock at the slip.

I lugged the two masts from *Molly B* down to the beach. They are quite a weight. At least it is downhill. I wheelbarrow all the rest of the rig to the slip where I repaired the punt.

This morning a large ship, the *Grey Seal*, lighthouse tender of the Irish Lights Service, arrived off the beach. A fine sight. It was met by two men in a currach from Corraun. The *Grey Seal* anchored and a party went to inspect the lighthouse, landing at the Light House Steps. The *Grey Seal* is a 200-foot behemoth with an massive helicopter pad perched above its bow. It makes an impressive sight anchored out in the bay.

Friday, April 29

The *Grey Seal* is gone by morning. Got going early, catching the 8.00 a.m. high tide. It's a bit of a logistical puzzle to put the *Molly B* back together. I collected the rigging and the punt at the slip, then went around to the beach and collected the two masts and lashed them on to the punt. I then motored the lot into the harbour in Corraun and unloaded.

I lay everything out on the pier. Masts, rigging, tools, ropes, spares. I rig the masts. As *Molly B* dries out on the dropping tide I am able to step both masts by canting them off the pier, me standing on a bollard. The main mast is the heaviest but it is stepped on deck so once it is jammed in its step I am able to balance, haul, push and coax it up with a series of rope pulleys and bits of string. The mizzen mast, lighter and shorter, is easier. The bowsprit, a clever Y-shaped design, slides into its position on the bow. When I make things I like them to be bolted together. Then it is easy to repair them.

It's a long day on Corraun pier, dashing about and getting it done. I am a man possessed. No one comes to bother me or interrupt the work. Job done, two masts solidly standing. When the tide returns that evening I motor back in the punt over the mud flats to Achillbeg, tired but triumphant.

Saturday, April 30

Up and into Corraun again on the early tide, much the same as yesterday, this time carrying the rudder and other gear. I get the rudder hung, a tricky job. The rudder is heavy but with the aid of a pulley and stays it slides into position and the stainless fittings pop into place.

I complete the running rigging, the ropes which control the spars and the sails. This involves shimmying up the mast many times. It's the cat's cradle of ropes and lines and bits of string that is the gaff rig of the *Molly B*. I am in a hurry all of a sudden.

It's time to get *Molly B* out of Corraun.

Chapter 14

I Am Going Far Away

Farewell to you my own true love
I am going far away
I am bound for California
But I know that I'll return some day
– Traditional

My journal continues for a further month. But the entries are short, cryptic and to the point. Not a lot of philosophising, soul searching or ranting. I was busy. I was excited to be leaving my island of broken dreams. There was much to do, and I had the bit between my teeth. I brought *Molly B* out from its winter refuge in the harbour at Corraun, anchored her off the beach in plain view from the windows of the house and she once again became the focus of my existence. This is how it played out – without the intrusion of daily entries.

It's a beautiful calm morning. Got over to Corraun at the top of the tide and hoisted sails on *Molly B*. It's a beat out of the small bay against the light wind. After two short tacks *Molly B* ran aground on the extensive sand flats outside the harbour. As the tide is falling

I have visions of sitting there for a whole tide – six hours or more. But I manage to pull the heavy hull off the sandbank with the punt and the motor. There were people watching the single-handed sailor doing his thing. I swallowed my pride, dropped the sails and towed all the way out to the mouth of the sound at Darby's Point. Here I hoisted sails again and sailed out to the beach at Achillbeg to drop the anchor.

Spent the rest of the day messing with the boat in a depressed feeling of déjà vu. 'Do I really want to get involved with that stupid, engineless, boat again?' I ask myself.

I paint a sign on the side of the boat:

Pete Hogan
Marine Paintings for Sale

Complete with a small palette logo. The plan is to sail around Ireland selling pictures. Back at the house I have a bit of a celebration. I even have a drink. It's a relief to be making a move.

There follows an anxious few days as the weather gods decide to play with me. The wind comes up from the east blowing directly on to the beach. The last thing I need now is for *Molly B* to be blown ashore or, far worse, on to the rocks either side of the beach.

I tie two anchors together in line and hope for the best. The wind screams across the expanse of Clew Bay and waves crash on to the normally sheltered beach. I cannot sleep at night. I spend it looking out the window into the darkness at the white breakers rolling in. I go down to the beach at dawn as *Molly B* holds on gallantly, bucking and pitching like a bronco in a rodeo. The beauty spot that is the beach on Achillbeg turns into a wild and dangerous place, like any seaside resort out of season when the wind blows. I simply have to wait and hope.

The wind swings around to the south and then a bit to the west. The danger is past.

I continue loading all my worldly possessions on board my floating home. My frying pan, oil skins, tools, books, radio, bits of string.

I go back to the house looking for my dreams. Now where did I leave them? In that drawer, at the back, under some stuff? No not there. Under the sink? Nah, I wouldn't have done that. In a box? Yes! Now where did I put that box? To make a long story short, I couldn't find them. They are probably still there, in that box, under something, on Achillbeg Island.

The weather settles. I decide to take a trip up to Westport. A sort of shakedown cruise. How nice to be off under sail again. I got under way at 12.15 and arrived at 15.30 anchoring on the mud flats not far from where Granuaile would have had her castle at Belclare, and where I had spent the summers of my childhood.

But as luck would have it, the wind came up strongly from the southwest and I remain stuck in Westport for three days. I stay on the boat anchored in the shallows. At half tide the boat bumps as it hits the bottom. Slowly it keels over to port or starboard as it settles in the mud at an acute angle. Automatically, I adjust my sleeping position as the hull settles on the bottom. Three hours later the water returns. The hull slowly lifts off, becomes vertical and then bumps gently as it floats off once more. All this I note in my half sleep. The natural order of things.

I do some shopping and a lot of visiting and saying 'thank you'. People are getting on with their lives and are not really in a holiday mode. Perhaps there is a message there. 'If you want to live on an engineless ketch anchored on a mud bank, go ahead and do it.' Vincent is busy with his salmon smoking business. My cousins are running their shop. People are less excited to meet the Artist on the Island. They are busy getting on with their lives. I should get on with mine.

I set sail as soon as weather permits and head back out through the muddy channels of Clew Bay. Past John Lennon's island and the lighthouse. I am lucky with the wind and reach Achillbeg without having to tack. Once again I anchor off the beach.

There remain a few things to be done to the house before I can leave. I attack the unfinished patio. It's a bit of a building site. So I make a big push there, leveling the mess of sand, gravel, broken bottles and flagstones into some sort of presentable order.

All the boat gear, half-finished artworks and drift wood treasures get moved out of the house. Furniture from the storage depot next door moves back in to its original location. Out with the studio, in with the holiday home. Somebody might want to use the house.

I have to finish Auntie Clare's crib set before I go. Work expands to fill time available. I chip away at Joseph and then at the Three

Wise Men and finally get the commission completed. I send it off. Auntie Clare loves her Christmas nativity set and it holds pride of place in her hallway, all year round, to this day!

I turn on the radio one morning. Mr. Dick Spring (Tánaiste and Minister for the Environment) is on the radio talking about the fact that he does not possess a 'magic wand'. He talks about spending £600,000,000 which is the estimate for his department. Sobering thoughts from the fella I used to play rugby with. He is getting on with his work; I should be getting on with mine. Staying on Achillbeg is not really an option.

Sighted the fox from the house down by the beach, moping around with its nose to the ground. The fox is getting on with its work. It's not dead yet. I would think that birds are the main victims of poison. Have not seen the choughs for some time.

I meet two sheep farmers, wandering around, tending sheep. We discussed the poison and they are a bit defensive. They seem to expect me to object to it but I do not. I'm the visitor here. I gave them a box to help them carry a weak lamb, which they have found, back to Cloghmore. It's good to be able to help even in a small way. They are getting on with their work, I should be getting on with mine. Staying on the island is not an option.

There remains much to be done to *Molly B* before I can leave. The winter storage, first moored to the slip on the island and then in the busy, crowded Corraun harbour, have been hard on the paint-work and the rubbing strip around the deck. There are repairs, dings, scratches and scrapes, some of them more than cosmetic. I do a huge overhaul on the kerosene stove which has brought me all the way from Vancouver. I should really dump it overboard. I spruce up the varnish work, I overhaul the sails.

I need to paint the underwater hull of *Molly B* with antifouling. To this end I tow her in to the pier at Cloghmore one morning on the top of the tide. It's a nice calm morning. The rest of the local fishing fleet have the same idea and are preparing to dry out so the pier at Cloghmore is a busy spot. Good progress scrubbing as the tide dropped and got more than one side painted on the tide. It will take two tides. I return in the evening with the tide and turn the boat around. I get back early the next day and complete the antifouling job.

A present from Martin Kilbane, who is also painting his boat nearby, of a fine crayfish. I sell a painting to Paddy Butcher. I think my 'Paintings for Sale' sign just might be working. Good old Paddy Butcher. He has always been friendly and supportive in a gruff, dis-tant sort of way.

Got a letter from Georganna. She is now in Switzerland. She says she might be coming back for two weeks! She had better hurry.

As *Molly B* is at Cloghmore and ready to go, I bring Pádraig and Darren out for a sail. It is the least I can do for Pádraig who has been very helpful over the winter. Darren has just made his first Holy

Communion. We reach along the shore to Mulranny and back. We end the sail by anchoring off the beach.

Pádraig died some years later, tragically young. R.I.P. Mary and Pádraig Kilbane were most helpful to me over the winter that I stayed in Achillbeg. *Go raibh maith agaibh.*

And then there is nothing really much stopping me from leaving. The house is closed. I leave the punt back over to Cloghmore and haul it up on the top of the tide. The fishermen and fish farm workers in Cloghmore are getting on with their lives. I should get on with mine. Staying on Achillbeg is not an option.

On the first of June I sailed away to the south in the engineless *Molly B.* Outward bound, around Ireland. Bye-bye, Achillbeg.

Afterword

'Where do we come from? Where are we? Where are we going?' This is the title of one of the most famous of Paul Gauguin's paintings. The big questions. I don't expect that he ever figured them out.

I was not sure where I was going but I certainly could not stay on Achillbeg island nursing a turf fire and going paranoid. My winter sojourn on Achillbeg had been some sort of bottom, or low point, for me. Certainly it was financially. When I left Achillbeg by boat that June day I had not a penny to my name. If I had wanted to leave by bus I could not have afforded to do so. Luckily, the wind is free. I sailed away in the engineless *Molly B*. 'It's all upwards from here,' I thought. 'It has to be.'

I cannot say I was sad to leave. Rather elated. You try something, it does not work, you try something else.

I was living on *Molly B*. She had been my home and my obsession for the last five years. The sign on the side of the cabin was my statement: 'Marine Paintings for Sale'. It was a discreet three-inch high sign on either side of the companion way.

That was what I wanted to do – paint pictures. I had a notion that I would sail around Ireland. So I set off, pointing the bow to the south. It was a sort of lap of honour, a way of getting back in touch with my Irish roots.

And longer term, what would I do? I did not really know. I thought I would head south in *Molly B* in the autumn, maybe to Spain, maybe the Mediterranean, maybe further. The whole world beckoned.